WHY SMALL BUSINESSES FAIL— DON'T MAKE THE SAME MISTAKE ONCE

William A. Delaney

Prentice-Hall, Inc.
Englewood Cliffs, New Jersey

Prentice-Hall International, Inc., *London*
Prentice-Hall of Australia, Pty. Ltd., *Sydney*
Prentice-Hall Canada Inc., *Toronto*
Prentice-Hall of India Private Ltd., *New Delhi*
Prentice-Hall of Japan, Inc., *Tokyo*
Prentice-Hall of Southeast Asia Pte. Ltd., *Singapore*
Whitehall Books, Ltd., *Wellington, New Zealand*
Editora Prentice-Hall do Brasil Ltda., *Rio de Janeiro*

© 1984 *by*

PRENTICE-HALL, INC.
Englewood Cliffs, N.J.

All rights reserved. No part of this book may be reproduced in any form or by any means, without permission in writing from the publisher.

Library of Congress Cataloging in Publication Data

Delaney, William A.
  Why small businesses fail--don't make the same mistake once.
  Includes index.
  1. New business enterprises. 2. Small business.
I. Title.
HD62.5.D44   1984   658'.022   84-11704

ISBN 0-13-959016-1

ISBN 0-13-959008-0 {PBK}

PRINTED IN THE UNITED STATES OF AMERICA

INTRODUCTION: LEARNING THROUGH OTHER ENTREPRENEURS' MISTAKES

This book is about small business. I don't know how to write about how to succeed because success is a subjective thing. It all depends upon your reasons for starting a small venture and your definition of success. You are a success when you say you are. Some start new ventures because they just are fed up and want to be their own boss. Sales, profit, growth, and expansion are of no interest in this case. Just the freedom to call your life your own and do what you want every day is enough. In that case, any one-man or one-woman proprietorship is a success. Others start new ventures with grand ideas to develop and grow into another IBM, GM, or U.S. Steel. Most of these entrepreneurs die off well before their "baby" grows and matures into the corporate giant they dreamed about. Some start new ventures because they have no choice. They suddenly lose their big job in mid-career and no one will hire them at their $100,000 per year salary, so they start up their own venture.

There is no "right" way to succeed. It is "right" if it is not immoral or illegal and you don't hurt anyone else while you succeed. What works once may never work again. Timing is vital and changing conditions, different people, and different opportunities make it impossible to ever duplicate any situation or to imitate anyone else. Also, the new ventures that succeed most brilliantly result from a brand-new idea that is unique. So, it is difficult to try to write about "how to succeed." Those that do tell about how they did it, but it is not so easy for others to read and do likewise. You are not them and times have changed.

There are, however, some things that are very common with new ventures and have had and will have similar effects upon many others, regardless of the type of company or venture you start or run. I'm talking about *mistakes*.

Wouldn't it be wonderful if you could read a "success cookbook" and follow the "magic recipe" step by step until, voilà, you too were up there with the big corporations? If you knew such a magic formula, would you take the time to write a book, or would you quietly follow it yourself first? If you knew how to make money in the stock market, would you do it for yourself or try to tell others how to do it? I shun brokers who call me and try to advise me to buy stocks that "can't miss." I always ask them if they are buying the stocks they want me to buy. They always hedge or say "No." They are assuring me of "success," but they get paid whether or not I succeed as a result of following their recommendations.

Success stories are great to read, but I wonder if anyone who reads about these successful people ever succeeds by imitating the famous author.

If that can't be done, then it does help to try to learn how not to fail. When a detective has five suspects and is unable to prove who did it, the detective may be able to eliminate four of the suspects and then concentrate the investigation on the one remaining. That does help. I will describe some errors and mistakes in this book so you can beware of them in your venture. Mistakes hurt; the only benefit you can gain from them is to learn a lesson so you won't repeat them. There are mistakes, and there are MISTAKES. Some, like lightning, strike only once. The same is true in the business world. The small venture, like the baby, is more vulnerable to mistakes than the mature firm. It learns while it grows, but some mistakes are

INTRODUCTION

deadly and, like lightning, you encounter them only once. You face bankruptcy or lawsuits or both, and it is all over.

In the pages that follow, I will describe some typical mistakes that many people who work in small ventures make, to their later sorrow. The examples given are all real, but the names are changed and small details are altered, because I am still living with and still paying for some of my mistakes. Please read on and avoid, if you can, these errors in judgment. The best way for anyone to learn from a mistake is to learn from someone else's blunders. This way you get the benefit from the lesson to be learned without the pain, expense, and frustration of making the mistake for yourself.

There are three ways to avoid mistakes. The first is to be so brilliant and lucky that you are able to figure it all out for yourself and go right along with no major problems. Few are so talented and fortunate. Next is to learn from others who have gone up the road ahead and sent back signals and information for your benefit. Finally we get to experience. It has to happen to you before you learn the lesson. Unfortunately, most of us choose experience as our teacher. It is a very good teacher, but is not forgiving or tolerant. The tuition to attend the school of experience is very high, because you do not learn the lesson until it is all over. The price of gaining such information is sometimes too high. Some, unfortunately, do not even learn from their mistakes. They just repeat them over and over and refuse to learn.

This book is intended for those who choose the second method to try to avoid mistakes. The first group does not need it. The learn-by-experience group has already learned the lesson and those who choose to repeat the same mistakes won't last long enough in business for anything to help them.

Let me repeat for emphasis, there are some mistakes that are deadly. They set up a chain of irreversible events that relentlessly follow, one after the other, like falling dominoes. In these cases, the best solution is preventive medicine or "don't make the same mistake once." Once is too much! Some mistakes are killers, and you do not get a second chance. If you inadvertently step off a cliff, you immediately know that you have made a mistake, but gravity takes charge and that is that. Others in line behind you stop and reverse direction. They learned the lesson at your expense. It is the same in business. Read on; you may learn some things not to do and how to avoid some fairly typical mistakes. That may keep you going until you are able to grow, survive, and achieve success in your endeavors, for whatever personal reason you have or whatever goal you want to reach.

William A. Delaney

ALSO BY THE AUTHOR

How to Run a Growing Company
30 Common Management Mistakes
So You Want to Start a Business!

CONTENTS

Introduction:
Learning Through Other Entrepreneurs' Mistakes v
1. What Exactly Are Your Chances? 1
2. Things to Do and to Avoid Doing in Planning 13
3. Ownership: Your Most Critical Choice 29
4. Structural and Legal Mistakes You Must Avoid 45
5. Steering Clear of Financial Pitfalls 67
6. Beware of These Seven Operational Wrongs 85
7. Preventive Remedies for Growth Pains 105
8. Ten Steps to Disastrous Mergers 121
9. How to Go Public with Style 138
10. Learning from Mistakes, Watching for Luck 155
11. Persistence and Good Judgment:
    The Winning Combination 167
12. How and When to Bail Out 185
13. Delaney's Business Laws and Guidelines 195
14. Recognize Mistakes and Benefit from Them 199

Index 205

1

WHAT EXACTLY ARE YOUR CHANCES?

THINK AHEAD

THE THOUGHTFUL PERSON, before starting on any trip or venture, thinks ahead and ponders the chances of reaching the desired goal. Before you go on a motor trip, you get road maps, plan out each day's driving, make advance reservations, or call ahead to relatives or friends to arrange where you will spend each night along the way. If you don't, you stand a very good chance of sleeping by the side of the road, running out of gas, getting lost, or worse. Everyone plans things like this well in advance, and also considers what they plan to do while on vacation and how much they plan to spend. We all plan out these little things, but do we plan out the big things? We certainly should, but unfortunately many do not because it is difficult to do. The more you try to plan the "biggie," the more unanswered questions arise.

Perhaps the most important career decision anyone can make is to start up a small venture or to join one already in existence. Should you leave your comfortable and fairly secure job in the big company and go into the small venture? What are the risks? What are the potential rewards? What do you, personally, stand to gain or lose? Is the reward worth the risk? Let's discuss some small business statistics, good and bad, so you can decide for yourself if you want to join the battle, because it really is a battle and not a game. In games, many times there are prizes for effort. You can get second prize or third prize, and that is not bad at all. However, as in a battle, in the small business it is

WHAT EXACTLY ARE YOUR CHANCES?

winner take all. No reward for effort, no second prize. You try and you win or you lose. Please know this before you jump in. It is sink or swim.

It is an entirely different world when you are on your own. No boss, no meeting you must attend, no unwanted trips that take you away from your family. You can do it all your own way, when and how you please. Sounds wonderful, doesn't it? But, before you jump in, let's look at some small business statistics so you may know what you are getting into. It is not all "beer and skittles," so please read on and then decide if you want to take the trip. The potential rewards are great, but so are the risks. You can't make a 100 percent insured investment and expect a 50 percent annual rate of return. You already know that. Big returns come with uninsured investment. So, be ready for risk and uncertainty in the small business world.
Here we go!

NICE STATISTICS

In the *Wall Street Journal* (8 November 1982, p. 32), J. Fred Kubik reports, "Small business owners sometimes make far more than Fortune 500 chiefs. Some guys are worth a hell of a lot of money. Just because it is a small business doesn't mean it can't be highly profitable and tougher to run than General Motors." Many of us try each year. David Gumpert, associate editor of the *Harvard Business Review*, in his article "Manager's Journal" in the *Wall Street Journal* (27 September 1982), reports that approximately 600,000 new ventures were started in 1981, recession or not. That number is double the rate of just ten years ago. Hopes spring eternal and each year the number continues to grow.

1. The *Wall Street Journal* (11 January 1982, p. 29) reports one small business for every 50 residents of the United States. If we assume a population of 230 million, that comes out to be 4.6 million small businesses. If we further assume eight employees per company with a

spouse, a couple of kids and assorted older relatives living with them, we can compute the astonishing number of over 150 million people working for or living off the small business. That is 65 percent of our total population. The small business is a major economic factor in our country.
2. An MIT report states that the majority of new inventions and innovations come from companies with 20 or fewer employees.
3. Two-thirds of all new jobs created in the past ten years came from the small business community.
4. *Electronic News* (29 March 1982, p. 1) reports 99.8 percent of all businesses in the U.S. are small, 47 percent of all nongovernment employees are in small businesses, and 38 percent of the entire U.S. Gross National Product comes from small business.

So, if you decide to start your own venture or join one, you are in some pretty good company. The chances to become wealthy are there. It is almost impossible for you to become wealthy working for someone else. Comfortable, yes, but wealthy, no. The income taxes on $1 million will take away at least 50 percent (it used to be 70 percent). State taxes may remove another 10 percent or so. Capital gains taxes are far lower (20 percent or so right now), so you can see the value in making it via ownership in your new venture. Also, salaries for successful small business people can grow rapidly, as Kubik reported. A key employee in a small venture can see wages and perks rise dramatically and very quickly into the six-figure category very early in life. It is all there for the taking if you can do it. Great! Now let's discuss the negative statistics.

NOT SO NICE STATISTICS

What happens to the 600,000 or so new businesses that start each year? Within one year, approximately 50 percent are gone. Within five years, 80 percent have folded. Of the 20 percent that survive, many are acquired by larger outfits. This benefits the owners only. The employees whose salaries and perks rise rapidly find it all ends as the new company puts its own "reasonable" salary and wage policies into effect. If you go out eight to ten years, you are down to a survival rate of about 5 percent or so, or to put it another way, 95 percent of small ventures do not survive eight to ten years. From 1980 to 1981, bankruptcies increased by 32 percent with small businesses having the lowest survival rate.

Why would any sensible person go into a situation that shows a 90–95 percent failure rate? There are as many reasons as there are people. As said earlier, some just have to do it. They are the entrepreneurs who thrive on risk and gambling. Some can't work for anyone but themselves; some are thrown into it and have no other choice. So, for whatever reason, 600,000 or so try each year with high hopes. Most are unprepared for what follows.

What happened to the majority of these outfits? They had a good idea or new product. Somehow they got started but fell by the wayside. In the big impersonal world of macroeconomics, the story is easy to identify and explain. It is called economic Darwinism: the survival of the fittest. In the pursuit of business, sales, and profit, the successful grow bigger and stronger at the expense of the smaller, weaker outfits who fall away and thus leave the market to those who survive and prosper. It is great for the winners and not so good for the losers. However, the alternative of a government controlled society, in which the economy is controlled by direct government intervention, creates an even worse situation. With all of our imperfections, I think few will argue that the free-market system that exists in the United States has resulted in the biggest and most successful economic system the world has ever known. No other country comes even close. Even though we have many things to correct within our own system, we shouldn't try to imitate other systems that produce a very low standard of living for their citizens, with no way for individuals with initiative, ability, hard work, and persistence to improve their own personal situation, and in so doing also create opportunities for others to benefit as well. I think that is a step in the wrong direction.

Napoleon, at the height of his power, dismissed Great Britain as "a nation of shopkeepers." Yet, these shopkeepers brought Napoleon down, when push came to shove. They had a better system. The freedom to succeed also is the freedom to fail. We have to have a big or "macro" system in which we will work at the "micro" or small level to try to do our thing, live our lives, and succeed or fail on our merits with as little interference or disruption as possible. I am by no means advocating the *laissez faire* system with all its imperfections and miseries, but I am afraid you will find when and if you embark on your new venture, the government is by no means a friendly ally. You will have to quickly learn how to deal with a blizzard of forms, procedures, and legalities to stay in business. You are considered as an "ongoing business" from day one, and you must conform to any and all laws and procedures.

There are small business organizations that can greatly help you in the early stages. The Small Business Administration (SBA) was established to aid and assist entrepreneurs during their difficult early years. The SBA was of great help to me with advice and information, and I strongly suggest you visit the SBA early (before you even start your venture), and pay close attention to what they tell you. They won't do it for you, but they can and will guide you through the early years. That is their job, and I found what they advised and the information they put at my disposal was invaluable. My company would not have survived without it.

PRODUCT EXPERTS

The typical new entrepreneurs have some new technical idea or product they know all about. Generally they have no, or very little, business or management or sales interest and/or experience. Wherever they worked before, these things were done by others and they were free to concentrate only on one leg of the business triad, the technical work. It is truly amazing how really naive such highly qualified, technical personnel are. I well remember a brilliant Ph.D. talking to me about funds for his project. He told me to charge it to overhead, and when I asked him if he knew what overhead was, he said it was something that was not direct labor. He had no idea what it was and no interest in listening to my explanation. Many like him end up in their own small business and are unable to control the flow of funds because they are unaware of one of the most important factors in business. How much do you charge for your product or service, and how much profit do you make as a result?

It can be seen that starting a new venture or working in one can be risky. This is not to say that working elsewhere is risk free. Statistics show that risk lies everywhere in big or small outfits, even in working for the government. Recent cutbacks in taxes at state and local levels have resulted in the mass release of many government employees such as teachers, police officers, and firefighters, who thought they had job security for life. Also, many giant corporations that have been adversely affected by the recent recession released many thousands. Personally, I don't think it is any more risky to work for a small rather than a large company. It all depends upon where you work and how good you are.

NO SECURITY: DOES THIS BOTHER YOU?

If you accept the fact that there is no real security this side of the grave, and you believe that your "job security" rests between your ears, then risk is not a factor to weigh heavily in your decision to start or work in the small venture. If, however, your skills are not transferable to another company or your value exists in solely what you know and do where you work now, or you owe your current situation to seniority with your pension just five or ten years away, then think it over. The decision is yours.

Some ugly statistics exist about those nice pensions too. Please look into them before you stay in a job you don't like, that bores you and leaves you unfulfilled every day. If you are hanging on there for the pot at the end of the rainbow and suffer through or tolerate an unhappy job situation for years, until you catch the "brass ring" on the day you retire, you are taking a risk. Please look into how many people live beyond two years after retirement. The number who quietly pass away might alarm you. If, however, you are working in a job you like, and you enjoy what you are doing, at least you are not sacrificing yourself or leading an unhappy or unsatisfactory existence for the reward that never comes. Are you also aware that the divorce rates rise too after retirement? When Hubert Humphrey was defeated in his bid for the Presidency, he went home for a while before he reentered politics. A reporter asked Mrs. Humphrey if she enjoyed having her husband home all day long. She replied, "I married him for better or worse, but not for lunch."

RISKS VERSUS REWARDS

In summary, we have to admit that the odds for any new small venture's surviving beyond a few years are small. On the other side of the ledger, however, the rewards for those who survive and grow are very great. Is the risk worth the potential reward? That is for you to decide and don't let anyone else do it for you. It is your life, your choice, and you live with your decision whatever it is. What could be fairer than that? Like any good risk taker though, you should know what you are getting into, what your goal is, and when you will reach it. What will you call success? Too many drift into this situation with little if any forethought or plans and later pay the price. You would not risk $1,000 to win $1, would you, even if the odds are heavily in your favor? That would be foolish.

If you study the statistics, weigh the odds, plan your moves carefully, and use your own good judgment, you will greatly enhance your chances for success. Far too many who establish a small business do so with little thought and no plans. They are poorly prepared for what is sure to follow and they are thrown by the first unanticipated problem that they encounter. I well remember what the first man I spoke to at the SBA in Boston told me. He said many come in with advanced degrees

WHAT EXACTLY ARE YOUR CHANCES? 9

from the local universities with big ideas about some new invention they want to patent. They want to start a business, go into production, and quickly become millionaires. After a few questions and a brief discussion, the SBA official knew they would never make it. He told me they all were brilliant technical people who were smart enough to figure out the answers to almost any question, but he went on to say something I have never forgotten. He said, "It's worse in their case, because it is not that they do not know the answers, it's because they don't even know the questions." That was in 1964 and since then I have seen it happen too many times to count. It is difficult enough to solve your problem when you know what it is, but in cases when you are feeling the adverse effects of a problem and you don't know what it is, or worse, you are solving the wrong problem, you have a 0 percent probability of correcting the situation.

Permit me to explain by two true situations what happens when you make the mistake of working on the wrong problem.

Some years back, a former associate came to me because, on his own with his own time, money, and effort, he and several associates had built a remote terminal plotting device. This was about ten years ago, and these devices did not exist then. His device was working, and he was ready to go. He tried to sell it to his technical colleagues in other big companies. They admired his demonstrations, but nothing happened. He wondered why the world did not clamor for his new device. He asked me what to do. He had done no market research. He did not know what that was. He had worked for several years in his cellar developing his new device. He was reinventing the wheel. A major corporation soon after announced a very similar new device, and sold thousands, via its marketing system that was already in place. His was better, he had it earlier, and it was less expensive and more reliable. He had not addressed the right questions to answer and solve. He remained in his job and has never again tried the small business route. He should have done his market research first, learned the statistics, potential market, and rate of return. He was very brilliant and could easily have acquired and understood this data, but his mistake was ignoring it. He never even thought about such things.

The second case is even more unfortunate. Two Ph.D.s left a big company to start their own consulting firm, based on one job that they got through a colleague they knew from old college days. Both worked hard and did an excellent technical job on their first job. It took 18 months to complete. One came to me, since my company was in its early years, and growing slowly but steadily. He said, "Bill, what's the secret?" He thought there was some secret magic formula to getting new work. He thought doing the best possible job for his client would lead automatically to more work than he could handle. How wrong he was. Again, no marketing or sales. As a Ph.D., he thought that sort of thing was demeaning and below his exalted status. He said he could not go out and do such things. He did nothing else, so he ended up returning to his former place of employment, where he still works. Once again, how right my SBA advisor proved to be.

CAUSE AND EFFECT

When a business person is seeking a loan from the bank, the reason that he wants the money is vital. If he needs the money, that's bad. Even though banks want to lend out money and they make their profit that way, you are very likely to be turned down if the bank officials conclude that you absolutely need the money in order to stay in business. You are denied the loan and you conclude you went under because you ran out of money and the banks would not give you the loan until things improved for you. In such a case, running out of money is not the problem. Your frantic seach for loans is addressing the wrong problem. You have a problem in your operations that is causing you to run out of money. Your sales are down or costs have risen too quickly or your accounts receivables are unpaid. The loan is treating the effect, not the cause, of your problem. See what is meant about not knowing the right questions to ask?

WHAT EXACTLY ARE YOUR CHANCES?

If the bank official grants you the loan to tide you over with no questions asked, then, in all likelihood, you will return a few months later with the same problem, only worse. Now, not only are you unable to pay off the old loan, you need a new one, because once again you are running out of money. You did not correct the cause of your negative cash-flow problem. The best way to get a big loan from any bank is to prove to them that you don't need it. You just want it. In that situation, you can get all you want and on very favorable terms, too, because they believe you are good for it.

Honestly now, would you personally lend out your money to someone who told you how desperately it was needed to stave off financial disaster? If you do, plan to never see it again. Business loans are not arranged because you need them and you will be hurt personally if you don't get them. Never tell a bank officer a tale of woe or how much you need a loan or you will go under. I would not give anyone a loan under those circumstances, would you? For a friend or relative, you'd make a gift maybe, because you won't get it back. But in the business world, a loan officer is judged by how much money he earns for the bank, not by how many needy people he helps out with other people's money. Don't thank them for giving you the loan. They don't give you anything. They sell it to you for the interest you pay. They should thank you for doing business with them. Keep that in mind. You also stand a much better chance of getting the loan from the bank president rather than from the loan officer who is under orders to grant no loans without 100 percent security for repayment.

Do you think when a bank grants a ten million dollar loan to any company that the company officers have to personally pledge any security? Absolutely not! It is done with statistics. They review your P&L and balance sheets and your written plan on what you plan to do with the money. If the statistics look good, you get it; if not, you don't. Many a very big loan has gone quietly down the drain with no one who was personally involved on either side losing one penny from his or her personal assets. This is how it works. Also, the more you bo row, the lower your interest rate will be. The trick is to get yourself quickly into the big loan category.

NUMBERS ARE IMPORTANT

Statistics matter. You should study and learn from them and use them as you think best. The reason why I discussed borrowing and running out of money early on in this book is many small outfits go under due to lack of sufficient funds to stay in business. Even after they failed, many still thought the reason was they ran short of cash. They still did not understand this was not the real problem; it was the effect of another problem within their company that caused their failure. This is a common mistake, so don't let it happen to you.

If you decide to take the small business route and fight the odds of survival, please remember to isolate, identify, and correct your real problems, and do not spend your time and efforts trying to temporarily correct the effects of your real problem. A company that is operating at a loss or running low on funds is bleeding to death from an open wound. A blood transfusion by itself without closing off the wound is temporary. It just flows into the corporate vein at one end (via loans) and flows right out the open wound at the other end. This all sounds so simple and easy to grasp, one wonders why it goes on every day in the marketplace. It is due to management mistakes.

Let's proceed to discuss other management mistakes that are common and can and will occur in any business, at any place, and at any time, unless the owners, executives, or managers are aware of them. Many can be anticipated and avoided. Prevention is better than cure as we all know, so let's get into some medicine, before the pain drives you to the doctors, it is too late to help you except to give and wish you lots of luck. At that stage, ve to stave off disaster.

2

THINGS TO DO AND TO AVOID DOING IN PLANNING

THE WORST PLAN IS NO PLAN

THIS CHAPTER FOCUSES on mistakes made in planning. The worst mistake anyone can make is to have no plan. Even a bad plan is better than no plan, because it is written down, can be reviewed and criticized, improved upon, and modified. It is easier to criticize than it is to create, so that is why many who start small ventures have no formal plan, but just a hazy, fuzzy idea of what they want to do. Remember, if you are unable to quantify your ideas and dreams and reduce them to a piece of paper, how in the world can you expect anyone to help you accomplish your "plan"? We can't get into your head, can we?

The business schools teach the management functions as (1) Plan, (2) Organize, (3) Direct, and (4) Control. Each is important, but they come in the order given. Any organization that tries to direct and control something that was poorly planned will fail. No amount of effort, dedication, hard work, or devotion can ever turn a bad or nonexistent plan into a good plan. Since the plan comes first, it is top priority. A good plan does not automatically result in a successful effort, but a bad plan or no plan guarantees failure, sooner or later.

Everyone has a dream. The trick is to make it happen. That is where planning comes in. It is very difficult to plan, because you are dealing with abstract ideas, concepts, future possible events, trade-offs, and alternative options. Also, the very fact that you prepared a plan can, in itself, alter the entire situation. It is a dynamic situation and conditions are changing while you

THINGS TO DO AND TO AVOID DOING IN PLANNING 15

do your planning. Some planners get too involved in the abstract or the future and depart from reality because they overlook some mundane item which was obvious to all but the planner.

I read an amusing story about a large Catholic university that planned to put up a new dormitory. Pro forma procedures required that the cardinal in whose archdiocese the college resided be informed of the new building and that the project receive his approval. Approval was always automatic, but in this case, back came the big envelope with the words "Rejected. Are they angels?" written in big letters across the master plan. This stopped the action dead in its tracks. A hurried call to the cardinal's residence resulted in an immediate revision of the plan. The cardinal's aides could find no men's rooms in the plan for the dormitory. Mistakes in planning, as you can plainly see, can be very serious. If passed unnoticed, the effect of poor planning can be difficult to reverse months or years later, no matter how efficiently you implement the plan. So, it behooves you to make a plan as best you can before you start.

WRITE IT DOWN

What are some typical mistakes some make in planning a new business?

As stated earlier, the worst possible plan is to have no plan. You just drift into it, go on from day to day and never know what is happening. This is known as the Columbus method. He didn't know where he was going; he didn't know where he was when he got there; he didn't know where he had been when he got back. This may be OK for adventurers and explorers, but hardly a good method for starting out on a new business venture. Yet, many actually go into business with no plan. Also, it has been estimated that approximately 85 percent of those who start new businesses each year cannot read or understand a Profit and Loss and balance sheet. They never heard of them. How do they plan anything? The answer is they don't. They end up like the inventor who is losing $1.00 on each widget sold. The inventor thinks, "That's OK, I will make it up in volume of sales." Some plan! Let's proceed now into some mistakes we can make in preparing our business plan.

BE FLEXIBLE

A plan deals with the future and no one knows what the future will bring. In the military, they say,"No plan survives the shock of battle." The plan must be flexible and capable of being directed and controlled. The feedback from the lower levels must be quick, clear, and concise, so the action can be altered to fit the plan or the plan altered to fit the action. A rigid and inflexible plan generally breaks down in later operations. No one is that good to be able to make one plan and see it unfold exactly as prepared with few, if any, disruptions. If you ever make a plan and your progress reports state that all is well and on schedule week after week, there are two possible explanations. The first is you are a genius. The second is you are not being told about what is really going on where the action is taking place. Only you can decide which of these two situations is occurring, but I think I know. It is the second one in 99.9 percent of the cases.

Yet we find many situations in which the plan, once completed, becomes the bible and cannot be changed when reality departs from the plan. The planner's ego gets into the act; watching a beautiful plan undergo change and modification is just too much to bear. How can any subordinate (who knows what is really going on) know more about it than I do? I am the boss, and what I say goes, even though it is not the correct thing to do.

In 1940, the French had a master plan to fight World War II with World War I methods. The Germans attacked; at French headquarters (can you believe this?) there were no telephones, so the master planners would not be disturbed. They stood in remote, lofty isolation with the inflexible master plan, and it was all over in six weeks, except to arrange for the surrender. That was not in this plan, was it?

More recently, I read about a multi-story library that was under construction. Some of the construction gang had some questions they wanted to have answered about the master plan. They were told to proceed and get it done. It was completed on schedule, but they discovered they could not put any books on the floors above the second level. The framework was for a building to house people, not books, and the weight of all of those books could not be placed on the upper floors. So much for the inflexible master plan.

Going to any extreme is bad. Having no plan is bad, and, at the other end of the spectrum an inflexible plan is almost as bad. If you are a planner, do not forget that the job is not done when you finish your plan. That is really just the beginning. You still have to do the job and your plan will change as you work. Either you make these changes in your master plan or someone else will make them for you, with or without your knowledge, by necessity. There are few things in life I can say without fear of contradiction, but one is, in a small business venture, change is the name of the game. You had better plan on it, because it will happen to you whether you plan on it or not. In a small business, a new job can double your sales base in a week. Are you ready for it or do you turn it away because it was not in your plan? Do you jump at it, take on a job you cannot do, and run out of working capital because you expanded too quickly? In most situations, the small business jumps at the chance for sudden and rapid growth. It is too difficult to turn down any new business opportunity, however the original business plan did not cover such a case. Now you are on thin ice.

PLAN AGAIN

An immediate new plan is in order, and if your plan indicates you cannot finance the rapid expansion required, then, as difficult as it may be, the best option is to refuse and grow via your plan. I have seen more than one outfit go under by reaching too far, too fast. The end came when they had insufficient funds to cover their payroll. This is easy advice to give, and difficult advice to follow. Any company, sooner or later, makes mistakes and has an unhappy customer now and then, however with a young emerging company, any difficulty of this nature with a client may jeopardize your survival. Even if you do survive, your reputation suffers and it may be a long time, if ever, before you get a similar opportunity to try again.

Trying to grow too quickly is a common business mistake. One outfit held to its original master plan, but raced out to get immediate loans to finance a big, new job. Several months later, when cash started to run out, it was determined that the rate of interest on the loan was higher than the rate of profit for the new job. In effect, the company was committed to do a job at a loss, just to grow quickly. Growth or size does not necessarily produce profit. Again, this is a fairly simple thing to understand, but you might be surprised to find how many small and even some big companies, I might add, unknowingly commit themselves to such a situation. Profit does not automatically follow growth. You have to plan it.

ANYONE CAN DREAM—THAT'S EASY

Another mistake one can make in planning is to produce an unrealistic plan. In this case, the planner is up in the clouds, and comes up with a marvelous long-range plan that has no possibility of fruition. This planner created a "wish list," rather than a workable business plan with a probability of success. I know that anything is possible, but don't plan on what is possible. Plan on what is probable! It is possible for you to win the state lottery when you buy a ticket, but I caution you against planning the one million dollar prize into your family budget for this year, or borrowing against your future winnings. The way to avoid unrealistic planning is to involve those who will later have to carry out the plan in the planning phase. This has a number of advantages:

1. You won't go off onto "Cloud 9" by yourself.
2. You get input from people with different points of view, i.e., financial, production, marketing, and others.
3. People feel more committed and motivated to implement a plan that they had a part in creating. Forcing a plan on your employees who do not like it or who

think it can't be done is heavy going, because you put them into a situation of proving themselves wrong later by working to make the plan succeed. Few people are strong enough emotionally to handle this situation. I have seen people later deliberately sabotage a plan that was working despite their prior predictions of "it couldn't be done." Their egos were so strong they had to make the plan fail in order to prove they were "right" earlier in the game.

I know of a part owner of a business (let's call him Joe) who did this, even though it almost put his company under. He actually "forgot" his ownership position and severely damaged his company, because he was forced to do a job he did not think could be done. It eventually was done, but he had to be removed from managing the job, because the president, who was the master planner, had not included him in the early planning stages. As part owner, this fellow felt "slighted" by being overlooked in the planning stage and later did great damage on the job. He even went to the client and tried to change the plan that was working and satisfying the client. As incredible as this sounds, it was the client who alerted the company president to this unfortunate situation, because the client was very happy with the plan as it was unfolding. The client, who dealt directly with Joe on the job day by day, saw Joe in action and listened to him complaining and trying to twist and alter a well-functioning business plan, simply because he had not been involved in its initial development.

4. If you can get a review of your plan by disinterested parties, this helps too. If you have a good board of directors, who do not work with the master planner, you can get more objective and realistic evaluations. This is sometimes easier said than done, because in the small business, the master planner usually is the president, who also owns a substantial part, if not all, of the company. In this situation, the board members know they can be removed at any time and they like receiving

their nice $300 a month or so for a few hours at the board meeting. In this situation, many board members are reluctant to voice objections; but if you are strong enough emotionally and you tell them it is OK to disagree with you, then you may get some who will take you at your word and tell you what they really think about your plans. It is well worth doing although it does, on occasion, bend the ego out of joint.

TOO MUCH PLANNING IS AS BAD AS NOT ENOUGH

The highly detailed plan is another mistake. Not as common as other planning errors, but common enough to mention at this stage. Overly detail-oriented planners generally are very knowledgeable about the subject. To demonstrate their deep understanding of the subject, the plan is right down to the "gnat's eyebrow." It is a thing of beauty. All who read it marvel at the depth of understanding and hard work that went into it. Nothing is left to chance. It is all there to unfold as time goes on. The effect of a too detailed plan is much like the rigid plan. It reduces the ability to react and change things. Also, it removes decision making responsibility at the lower level. Most people like to be told what you want done and when, but don't tell them how to do it. They generally know how to do it better than you do anyway, so the plan should not get into too much detail. If it does, it requires too much study and discussion at the lower level. At that level, you want action rather than too much study and review of the plan.

With an overly detailed plan, lower-level managers tend to follow it to the letter. Everything is in the plan so all they have to do is follow it in detail. They don't have to think or plan their own small piece, so they won't. Initiative and many good ideas and improvements get lost this way. There is no freedom to think or change anything. The cookbook philosophy takes over. Do what it says, shove it in the oven, and as long as you followed the recipe, you are not responsible for what comes out later. If it is good, the master planner did it, and if it is bad you can say "I only followed orders." Hardly a good training ground for young people with any initiative, is it?

Also, no plan is 100 percent correct. The more detail you put down, the more the plan will depart from reality. You don't want to get bogged down over too many minor items. You will though, if you try to plan in detail how to do everything. In this case, too many reports come back up the line requesting approval of deviations or modifications to the plan.

If you tend to plan in too much detail, you can improve it by having some others take your plan and make it less detailed. This is easier to do than having someone add to your plan, because, as said earlier, it is easier to criticize and edit than it is to create. In an overly detailed plan, you tend to plan how you would do it, but you are not going to do it, so leave it to the employees who have the direct responsibility to do their part. You will also save yourself a lot of time as well. In addition, if you are looking to the long range and you want junior and middle-level personnel to learn how to plan, let them do their little piece early on. You may find a gifted planner down in the ranks and you never would know he or she were there if you did it all yourself.

DON'T PLAN BACKWARDS: THE PAST IS GONE FOREVER

Planning for the past is another common mistake some planners make. This is by no means restricted to the small business. Napoleon said: "Most generals are busy preparing for the last war." Instead of looking forward and taking advantage of what is new, they think only in terms of former experience and try to project the past into the future. What worked before may never work again in the same way. These planners walk around with an answer looking for a question that will fit it. If no question fits their answer, they change or twist the question to fit their answer. For heaven's sake, don't plan backward, that is not what planning is. Planning is for the future. Use the past as a guide, not as a bible to reapply over and over again without change.

When you start a new venture, it is all new, and trying to use former methods or techniques from former places of employment may not work too well at all. Certainly you draw upon your education and experience, but you can't blindly repeat the lessons of the past. Nothing is ever the same twice. The planner must take this into account or else. We had to remove one of our senior staff from working on proposals to win new contracts. He constantly dealt in the past, and each time he tried to write a technical plan to match the client's needs, he would always first review former proposals and try to "cut and paste" the old material to match the new Statement of Work. He would twist and distort the Statement of Work to try to make it fit his plan from the past. We were unable to get him to change, so he no longer writes plans. Others do it and he implements them.

Everyone is not cut out to be a planner. Good planners are worth their weight in gold. If you try to run your own new venture and you cannot make a good plan, you are starting out with a disadvantage because you will have to leave that to others to do for you. This planner had better be treated well. Your survival may well depend upon his or her planning abilities.

ELEMENTS OF YOUR PLAN

What constitutes a good plan?

1. It describes the end goal.
2. It lists a schedule.
3. It has a budget.
4. It describes the general approach.
5. It has a staffing plan.
6. It is flexible and can be easily modified.
7. It describes the method of direction and control.
8. It is capable of quick response to changing situations.
9. The chain of command is clearly defined.
10. Specific authority and responsibility are defined.

11. A "safety valve" for emergency situations for direct communication to the top is established.
12. It deals in the future, not the past.

The company's master business plan should be in three parts. The level of sales you expect to reach is projected first. A second sales plan that is the highest you can ever hope to reach without drawing up an entirely new plan is then developed. Finally, a third plan with the lowest possible level of business activity that you can tolerate and stay in business is made. If these three plans are well done, you have a 60 percent to 80 percent chance your sales will fall somewhere between the lower and upper sales prediction. It will not fall on your best estimate line. No one is that good at predicting. This sort of plan has built in the ability to vary your response to fluctuating business conditions, so you can adjust rather than start or stop.

OBJECTIVE REVIEW

It is best to discuss your business plan with as many people as possible before you start. The SBA, professors, bankers, and other business people whom you know and who are willing to help and advise you are all good advisors. The best laid plans of mice and men oft go awry, but at least you know what your goal is and what the monthly or intermediate milestones may be. Long-range planning (five years or so) is not of much value to the small business. A good one-year plan is about as much as you can hope for in the early years. Even in large companies, the five-year plans are exercises in "science fiction." I know, I participated in them. How do you tell a planner what you expect your department's sales to be in four or five years, and list new potential clients and the probability of capture? We just gave them any number they wanted and went back to doing this year's work.

You will need a good business plan if you need start-up capital which you get from a bank. It will all be based on your plan and if they believe it. If they do, you get the loan; if not, you don't. Many companies that are easy to start and require no capital up front can be started with no plan, because you do not need one. You sort of ease into it. Software service companies are a case in point. You start with one job based on some personal contact you have. You go to work at the client's facility and you need little start-up capital. It is easier to start than a new production company that needs $75,000 up front to open the doors. However, in the second case, you must do advanced planning, whereas the small service company does not. The odds of survival are greater for the company that did the planning in advance.

The way you start out with your plan (or without one) is a very important factor in your later success, survival, or growth. In many cases, these plans are self-fulfilling prophecies in that what you plan is what you get. Rarely does a new company exceed its first-year sales plan. It is that or less, in most cases. The planning function forces you to think ahead and in so doing, all of the other things you must do and when to do them become apparent. Sometimes it is best to plan from completion backward. Set a date in the future and work backward from that date until today. If you come up with "negative time" (i.e., you find you need ten more months and you have only five), do it again and again until you don't. There are many techniques and devices to aid the planner, but to be realistic, the new venture cannot afford them in the early stages. Overly sophisticated procedures and techniques may lend beauty and neatness to the format, but little else. Also, the new venture tends to be informal and any planning done is usually restricted to one or several of the owners, so I won't go into the many and various tools that do exist. There is no point in describing to you the value and comfort of driving the Rolls Royce when you can't afford it. Pencil, paper, and rulers are all you really need. It is the quality of your plan that matters, not the beauty or format. Multi-colored slides and expensive charts and graphs can wait until you can afford them. Be neat though. You won't get anyone to lend you any money or to work on a plan that is written on the back of an envelope or on your desk pad.

I am aware of two extreme situations that bracket the planning problem. In one case, the owner told me that he has 100 people reporting directly to him. He is so busy he does not have time to eat. He regularly works a 70-hour week because he has no plan, so he cannot organize his group to implement the "nonexisting" plan. When he really needs the job done in a hurry, he told me he gives the same job to two teams and sees who gets it done first. It is amazing to report he survives and continues to get work from various clients. I have no idea how he prices up any job, but somehow he manages to do so. There is no way this fellow's company can grow much more. He does everything himself and he is running out of hours in the week. He has no plan to assign work or to delegate any authority to anyone else. His plan, if you would call it that, is very egocentric, in that he is involved in it all, day in and day out. I asked him what would happen if he got sick. He said he would have to recover very fast and that would be his incentive to get well fast. He can't grow much more, can he?

In the other case, this owner went overboard with planning. With thirty employees, he came up with seven levels of authority. That is more than in any big division. Planning meetings and coordination meetings took up most of everyone's day. I knew this owner quite well, and I tried to suggest that he was overplanning. No one could focus on the work, new business, and sales. He had everyone's eyes turned inward and downward. He survived three years and went under due to failure to complete a contract he had with a big client who took legal action against him. Last I heard, his former managers formed a new company without him and went back in after his old clients, and they are doing very well.

When he was trying to run his seven level company, I asked him why he planned so many levels for only thirty employees. He answered by telling me that was the way the company he left was organized. He had been working for a 10,000-person organization and he blindly imitated it. He even used the same titles for each management level. He obviously felt that imitation would make his outfit become the same as his former employer. That is the same as an art student's cutting off his ear and mailing it to his girlfriend in hopes that it will make him a great artist like van Gogh. Study and learn from other successful companies, but blind imitation, for no good reason, hardly seems very wise to me.

PLANNING IS DIFFICULT

Very few people are good planners, and if you are not one, then it is a good idea to hire one to work for you if you can. However, the good ones are generally so highly paid and well cared for wherever they work that you may not be able to afford them, at least not at the beginning when you need them the most. In all likelihood, you will be the planner and all will look to you for the leadership role in this very, very important function. It comes or should come first, and everything that follows should be oriented towards achieving some portion of your plan. Mistakes in the organization, direction, or control of your company can be harmful, but they are not critical, because if your plan is good, you are able to correct these problems by a change in personnel, priorities, or emphasis. An error in your plan, however (or worse, no plan at all), cannot easily be corrected by your organization or by direction or control.

If the plan has you doing the wrong thing, in the wrong place, and at the wrong time, there is absolutely no way that perfect organization or excellent direction can repair the situation. All that these other management functions can do is to quickly and efficiently turn out the wrong end product, because the plan was faulty. Many avoid planning, because it is very difficult to do it well. We all have the human tendency, when we face a difficult decision or problem, to busy ourselves with things of lesser importance that we know how to do well. It is good for the ego to do something well, so we do other things and say, "I am too busy to get around to that right now," when, if we face up to it, we are merely avoiding or postponing attacking the hard stuff, even though it may be the most important thing to do.

If you don't plan your new venture, you are in for heavy going later on, and you just stack the deck further against your chances for success. As you well know, the odds are against you, at best, without making additional mistakes to make matters worse.

KEEP TRYING

I am certainly no genius, not by a long shot, and I well remember making my first two-year plan. I must have done it 50 times before I got the one I liked, and two years later we were off the mark by 9 percent in sales, but on the high side, which did not bother me at all. If I can do it, so can you. So, make your plan first and don't stop until you get the one that suits you, then go and make it happen.

Recently I read about a very successful man who was entering government service at a very high level. His wife was interviewed and said he would do well in whatever job he got because he knew how to plan. She said when he finished graduate school, he told her where he planned to be by his 35th birthday, and he missed it by two weeks. Once again, if he can do it, why can't you? Don't give the planning function short shrift, especially in a new venture. You may not get a second chance this side of the bankruptcy courts if you do.

I am on the advisory board of a local university's Small Business Advisory Council. We meet quarterly, and at the last meeting the director was presenting statistics about the number of people the council had met with and assisted during the previous three months. The number was quite high, as far as I was concerned, considering the small staff they had. I asked how could the staff advise so many people. The director replied that the vast majority of people who come in ask how to get money to start up. The staff asks to see their business plans and they have none or something on a scrap of paper. They are asked if they would lend money to anyone who asked for it, but had no plan for what to do with the money. They all answered "No." This takes about five minutes. Next, they are told to come back and the council would spend time helping them make a basic business plan. They quietly leave and most never return. The council did a service for each and every one of these people. Business failure, in these cases, was almost an absolute certainty. I asked how many who came in had done any real planning at all. The answer was about one in a hundred.

The planning function is absolutely vital to the success of the small venture. Without it you leave things to chance and you find yourself reacting to events or situations created by others that affect you, rather than acting directly to execute your basic plan. Luck does have its place in the scheme of things, as we will discuss later (in Chapter 10), but don't leave everything to luck. No one is that lucky, or to put it another way, if you leave it all to luck, then some of the luck you get will be bad. The plan comes first and helps you to reach your goal, measure your progress towards that goal, and indicate when and where adjustments or corrections are required along the way.

3

OWNERSHIP: YOUR MOST CRITICAL CHOICE

ONCE IS TOO MUCH

NOW WE GET into the areas of serious and permanent mistakes. One mistake here is too much. These mistakes are either impossible to correct later, or, at best, very, very costly and difficult to correct. When you go into business with co-owners, you are getting married to them for better or for worse, for as long as your corporation lives or they sell out to you or someone else. Think twice, no think ten times before you take a co-owner into your business venture, or better still, don't take any at all if you can avoid it.

There are three basic types of business enterprises, the proprietorship, the partnership, and the corporation. Each is different and designed for different circumstances. Let's briefly discuss the first two and get to the corporation, where the real action takes place.

In a proprietorship, you own it all, and that is that. One-man outfits, "Ma and Pa" stores, and all sorts of small enterprises exist in which the owner works for him- or herself. There is a place for the proprietorship, but not for you, if you plan to grow into a bigger business. Your personal and business assets tend to be intermixed. That is OK if you remain small, but not if you expand and grow. Profit or loss is direct to the individual personally.

The partnership is what it says. Two or more people each own a percentage of the company. It is like a proprietorship, only

OWNERSHIP: YOUR MOST CRITICAL CHOICE

with more than one owner. I am not too high on partnerships. If there is a place for them in the business world, I can't see it. Here is why. Partners are liable for all debts of the company over and above their personal ownership position. This is risky business. If you have a partnership with four others, and you own 20 percent of the company, you get 20 percent of the profits. So far so good. If, however, there is a loss or you go bankrupt and the company owes $100,000 to its creditors and your four partners do not have $80,000 for their share of the debt but you do, guess what can happen. You personally can be required to pay the entire $100,000 if you have it. Hardly seems fair to me, and this reason alone is enough for me. I would avoid the partnership, but you may have some good reason for doing it. If you do, I wish you would write and tell me why, because I have never been able to figure out why anyone would want to go into partnership in a business venture and risk all of his or her personal assets if the venture goes sour.

Now we get to the corporation. This is the structure of most businesses that grow into any size. Now you need a lawyer. In the legal profession, they say, "Only God can make a tree, but only a lawyer can make a corporation." I am not a particularly big "fan" of lawyers, however like dentists and undertakers, they are necessary in the scheme of things. Lawyers are the only people I know who can outtalk me, and I like to talk, so they upset me when they continually beat me in a verbal duel. Your first order of business is to choose a good lawyer. A mistake made here is not apparent at the time, because some mistakes made at this early stage do not manifest themselves until years later. Then it may be impossible or very difficult to correct them.

Lawyers are specialists. If you make the mistake of using a lawyer who is not a legal expert in forming new corporations, stand by for trouble. Many entrepreneurs use their family lawyers or call some old college buddy who does the legal work at a very low fee for his old roommate. This is false economy. You "save" a few hundred dollars up front and get incorporated incorrectly, or your corporate bylaws are not right. Later these "little" oversights create corporate chaos or confusion or a great deal of lost time, effort, and money. Remember, just as there are medical specialists, there are legal specialists. Would you go to your old friend who is an eye, ear, nose, and throat specialist if you had trouble with your knee? Hardly; even if you did, he or she would quickly refer you to the proper specialist. If you make the same mistake with lawyers, they may not refer you to another lawyer, but try to do the job for you. Do you want an inexperienced lawyer organizing a corporation for you? Do you want to be a surgeon's first operation? The choice is yours. Think about that carefully.

SEEK ADVICE

Go to your local bank or to the American Bar Association and request a list of law firms that handle new corporations. Talk to several and ask for references. Call these company presidents and check out the lawyers or law firm who did the legal work at the beginning. The small business has a network, so tap into it. We all know we have to help each other, and other company presidents will openly and willingly tell you what you want to know. All you have to do is ask. We do help each other out since we know how tough it is to survive the first few years. Don't play false economy here. Get the best! It you later fail, it won't matter, but if you succeed and grow, it will be a very important factor in aiding or hindering your future efforts. In the midst of a dynamic expansion, when all eyes are on the future, it is tough to be pulled up short by a mistake or oversight made five or ten years back in your bylaws and you have to stop and correct it. Maybe it can't be corrected but now you have to live with it because of some legal technicality put in or left out by an inexperienced attorney who is long gone.

DO IT YOUR WAY

So, choose your legal counsel wisely. What's next? You develop your corporate bylaws. Don't let your lawyer use some other company's bylaws and just put in your company name. You already (I hope) have your previously prepared business plan. Now your bylaws are written to reflect your business plan. Ask for copies of many other companies' bylaws. Read them to learn the format, procedures, and what they say. Then make certain that your lawyer prepares a set of bylaws that you fully understand and that reflect your business plan. Sometimes it is difficult to later modify bylaws if you want to change into another line of work. Your bylaws may require board of directors' or stockholder's approval, and you may not be able to get it. Do not dismiss bylaws as something of little interest or importance to you. I did, and later I was badly burned. I let the lawyer draw up the bylaws on his own and later I discovered things in them that I did not like at all, and they are still there. I live with and work around them every day, but I can't change them. Don't make this mistake. It is too costly.

Next, we come to another decision that is permanent and cannot be changed later. Who is going to own shares in your new venture? A mistake made here is deadly. Whoever gets or buys a piece of your new venture owns it until he or she decides to dispose of it. Think about this before you portion out or sell the shares in your venture. Shareholders are exactly what the word says they are. They hold and own shares in your enterprise. Shareholders are almost partners. Keep total control if you can until you "go public." This will be discussed in Chapter 9.

A close friend who is an architect put up a beautiful office building with another architect on a fifty–fifty ownership basis (never go fifty–fifty with anyone, because no one is in charge when two or more are in charge). Internal bickering led the other fellow to sell out his 50 percent ownership to a third party. My friend offered $100,000 more than the other party, but hard feelings were present and his offer was rejected. In came Mr. "Gauche," who is driving my friend right up the wall. His new office building lies 50 percent empty and they fight every day over who is to blame. A simple buy/sell agreement could have avoided the whole problem that my friend must live with every day. He says he hates to go to the office now and stays away as often as he possibly can. What a mistake! It is too late now and my friend is looking for ways to sell out any way he can to keep his sanity. He counted on this building and its income setting him up for life, but peace of mind comes first and it is only a question of time before he sells out for whatever he can get. Don't let this happen to you.

GETTING THE MONEY

Any venture new or old needs money, and there are three ways to get it:

- Use your own personal funds.
- Sell shares in your venture.
- Borrow.

If you can use the first option, that is the best if you later succeed. You retain 100 percent ownership, and, as your company grows, you benefit the most. However, in most cases, you do not have sufficient funds available, or you don't want to risk all of your hard-earned savings or the house or the kids' college money. If you later fail, you lose it all. You may want to spread the risk. The choice is yours.

The second option, to sell shares in your new venture, may be necessary. Be careful if you do this. You may "give away the store" for a few thousand dollars today and live to regret it in a few years. Shares in new ventures are very risky since most fail, so you may have to sell a large percentage of your new enterprise to the "money boys," who buy into many companies on risk and look for the one big payoff. I know of a multi-million dollar computer company in which 55 percent of the company stock was sold at the start for $70,000. Some bargain, but you may have no choice if you need the start-up capital.

Be very careful you do not surrender controlling interest in your venture just to get going. If you do, the following scenarios can follow. If you later fail, no personal problem for you. You spent the $50,000 or so put up by the shareholders and it all went bust. It is over. No one argues at a funeral. If you succeed, however, and your venture prospers and grows and you do not own a controlling interest in it, stand by for a sudden and drastic change. I have seen it happen. The majority owners, who put up their money on risk, now assert their controlling position. They have a point. They put their money on a high-risk venture. It is now paying off, and they now want to call the shots. No one bothered you when you were working 80 hours a week to make it go, but now they choose a new president and company officers. You are offered a position of technical director and your expected salary and perks do not materialize. They don't need you that much any longer. They may be able to hire someone, who can better direct a ten million dollar annual sales company, and they may well be right. Those who start up new companies very often cannot run them well when they grow. Someone from Harvard Business School may be the better person at this point. If so, goodbye to you! You can prevent this from happening by a firm agreement made up front before it ever develops. I strongly suggest you think ahead to this situation. After all, you do want your venture to succeed, don't you? Plan also what happens to you, if it does succeed, because you don't have to plan what will happen to you if it doesn't. We all know what will happen to you in that case.

If you try to borrow, you have no corporate assets, accounts receivable, or retained earnings on your balance sheet, so you will most likely have to pledge your personal assets to back up the loan or bond you receive until your company itself can justify and finance its own corporate borrowing. I can't say whether or not you should do this, that is up to you, but one mistake here and you lose a lot more than just your business venture.

ATTRACTING GOOD PERSONNEL

Let's discuss a situation in which you don't have to sell shares in your venture, but you want and need certain key, highly talented individuals to work for you. You can't as yet afford the high salaries they demand. Why should they leave their good jobs in middle or higher management in a big outfit to work for you? You may have to attract them with a piece of the action right up front or with stock options. The first mistake you can make is giving the stock up front. I strongly recommend against this no matter how badly you want or need this person. No one is indispensable, especially someone whom you have not hired yet. Remember, if you give it up front, your employee owns a piece of your company now and you can't get it back unless you buy it, and he or she wants to sell it to you.

Consider this true situation. A fellow I know formed a small service company. He invited two of his former subordinates to accompany him. He divided the shares equally. As the company progressed due to the president's ability to sell and get new customers, the other two objected to the added work necessary to handle an expanding company. One quit for 18 months to rest and returned at his pleasure. The other continually badgered the president who continued to make the company grow over his associate's objections. All three split the profits equally. They approved equal salaries and perks for each other. The company is still growing and the three hardly speak to each other. Why? They were not able to grow as the company grew. New employees hold more important jobs than they do. The mistake was made and it is permanent.

HOLD YOUR STOCK

Don't give out stock to anyone in advance, and never give out controlling interest. If you do and if you succeed, you may live to regret it. One way to award stock and the problem of control is to consider two types of stock. There is a class of stock that is nonvoting. Shareholders own shares in the corporation, but they cannot vote. This is perfectly legal. All you have to do is set it up that way in advance. It is much to your advantage to do this, but many new entrepreneurs do not know about this and award fully voting stock to others when they don't have to do it.

Another factor to consider, in advance, is any stockholder has a right to see the books and records of the company in the annual report. After all, legally, the stockholder owns the company or at least part of it, and the company management works for him or her. The owner/employee has two distinct roles. One as an employee who is under the direction of the company president and another as stockholder for whom the president works. This can cause confusion in the minds of some people who cannot forget their ownership role in on-the-job activities. I have seen some openly insult and disobey the boss because they think, "you work for me, I don't have to do what you say." I have seen some refuse to take a necessary business trip or go home and pout for several days over a disagreement in the office, because they believe it is their company or at least part of it is, so they can do what they like.

Minority stockholders will learn what salaries the company officers are making and can disrupt stockholders' meetings by loudly objecting to the high wages and perks, because they want some too. Also, this information will become common knowledge among all employees if the owner/worker chooses to pass this information to others, and believe me, many choose to do this. Do you really want this sort of thing to go on? It won't get you any sales, won't increase your profit, and won't help the company grow. This is all bad for your company, especially during the early years. Who needs it? It can all be avoided by retaining the stock and not giving it to an employee, who is unable to understand or work with a new role that has two distinct and separate functions, one as part owner and the other as employee.

Please remember that the types of people whom you need at first to get started may not (and probably won't) be the same types you will need later on to rapidly expand and grow. The hard working, no nonsense, sleeves rolled up technical person is needed at the start. Later the polished, educated, sophisticated person, who speaks well and helps you market and win new clients is the person you may need. How do you get them later if you gave out too much stock too early to those who can run or build the product, but know nothing else, and want no part of sales, marketing, or keeping the books? They hate those jobs and always will.

Oddly enough, ownership troubles rarely develop when the company is struggling for survival. All work many hours, no extra pay, there's great cooperation, and the company survives and starts to grow. The profits roll in. The company president wants to retain the earnings for corporate expansion. His co-owners object. They want big dividends right now, and the battle is on. Corporate divorces kill off many a good small outfit that could well have survived. The owners started to fight amongst themselves over how to use the profits or who got the big salary raises. I have seen this happen. It almost happened to us, too. So, don't let this happen to you. Going public is an entirely different matter, as will be discussed in Chapter 9. The premature and excessive distribution of stock is a very serious mistake and is not easily corrected. I made such an error and when I want to see the one who caused the problem, all I have to do is go and look in a mirror and quietly mutter "stupid" to the face I see looking back at me. It is very ego shattering and it can't be corrected.

MOTIVES DIFFER

Do not assume that what motivates you will motivate others in a similar way. It is true that you can go around with a person of the opposite sex for years, but you will not know what they are really like until you marry them. You learn more about them in two weeks than you did in all the years you went with them prior to the marriage. It is even more difficult when you become co-owners, because one big factor is missing. You don't love each other so it is even harder to "forgive and forget" when the little and big disagreements arise. You will argue over what kind of furniture to buy or what kind of company cars to get because one owner has a brother who sells cars that you don't want to get.

I have seen co-owners refuse to work on jobs they don't like, assign heavy work to others and then go home and stay out for several days. One I know drives his associates crazy. He won't work on Monday or Friday afternoons, and is absent more than he is present, but, as a stockholder/employee, they can't do anything about it. They have to work around him. The employees work harder than he does.

OWNERSHIP CHANGES SOME PEOPLE

You would think that employees would work harder and have more personal interest in a company in which they own a substantial percent of the stock than for a company in which they are just employees. Unfortunately, this is not always true. Some who know they now have an ownership position in an ongoing company deliberately slack off, knowing their job is secure. The pay, job, and share of profits are all there, and no one can take them away. In response to this very fortunate situation, you find them giving less effort, taking more time off from work, and actually showing less interest in making the company grow. I have read about people who are paid excessive salaries for what they do (i.e., star athletes, movie or TV stars). Do they work harder the more they get or do they demand more and more for less and less efforts? I encountered the situation personally and, to my amazement, saw a formerly hard working, talented, and very nice person turn into a touchy, grouchy, overly sensitive individual who disappeared from his office and was a chronic late arrival and early departure problem. He did less and less work the higher his salary and perks went, due to his ownership in a successfully growing new venture. He did not want to work any longer.

Two psychologists I know have a very lucrative business. They are sort of "marriage counselors" to the owners of small privately held businesses. For a very large fee, they go in, interview the owners, and try to work out some method for these co-owners to get along with each other. The stories they tell are incredible; they show what people can and will do to each other, sometimes destroying the company as a result. I asked one of the psychologists how do you avoid or prevent this serious problem? He said, "Don't take on partners or co-owners."

OWNERSHIP PROBLEMS

In discussing this problem with other small business owners, I find general agreement that this situation is common enough to require a special warning to anyone who is thinking about awarding stock ownership positions to anyone too early on. There is also the added problem if the person becomes ill, dies, or leaves your company and goes to work for a competitor. Most small companies are closely held in that the stock is not sold on the public market so only a few individuals own the shares. This ownership position is based upon the "worker/owner" principle. Your salary, bonuses, and perks support you and you let the profits remain to finance expansion and growth. However, if the owner/worker falls ill and his or her salary stops, the demands for higher and continuing dividends grow out of necessity. What do you do? The death of the owner/stockholder puts the shares into his estate and his widow may sell them to anyone. Even worse, she may retain the stock, get a seat on the board of directors, and thus have an important voice in the control of your venture with no working contribution on her part. Naturally this person will look for high dividends and vote for any president who promises to deliver higher, immediate financial return, because she needs it now.

The voluntary departure of owner/employees is also a bad scene. They leave and go elsewhere, gaining from the future efforts of those left behind with no further effort on their part. A recent newspaper article described this sad scene. A family-owned company had been in business for many years. The father, in his attempts to avoid or reduce death taxes, transferred, over the years, a substantial number of shares of the corporation to his son. The son was about 25 years old and got married. Two years later a divorce followed and his wife got 50 percent of the son's stock in his father's business. They had to buy it back from the fortunate young lady to avoid her becoming an active member of the company's board of directors, due to her ownership position in this prosperous company. How would you like to have to buy back your own company stock because your son made a bad marriage?

OWNERSHIP: YOUR MOST CRITICAL CHOICE

Some foresight and planning can avoid or reduce mistakes in this area of corporate ownership. Some suggestions are:

1. Consider the stock as sacred as your family honor and integrity and hold it to yourself for as long as possible.
2. Never give away stock up front to anyone. Use the stock option. Make them earn it first by reaching some sales or profit goal.
3. Award money, perks, gifts, promotions, or any other incentive. Use stock where there is no other way. Many will take other incentives if you offer them.
4. Use the special class of nonvoting stocks so whoever gets stock cannot interfere with the way you choose to operate your company.
5. Have a buy/sell agreement for these owners/employees. If for any reason, i.e., resignation, illness, or death, they no longer work for your company, they must sell the stock back to your company at an agreed upon price. This agreement can be in force for a specific time period or until the company goes public or you reach a certain size in sales or accumulated retained earnings. This protects you from early departure of a key person who is so important to you as an employee that you awarded him or her stock in your venture. This employee's continued effort was the reason for the stock award or option in the first place. If he or she no longer works for you or becomes an ineffective employee, you have an escape route.

BUY/SELL AGREEMENTS

As a matter of fact, the existence of a good buy/sell agreement not only avoids trouble and interference from relatives of deceased former stockholders, it almost eliminates the possibility of owner/employees' taking it easy and coasting on the job. They know if they were ever fired for nonperformance, they would have to sell the stock back to the company at a price well below its current market value. In the case of illness or death, fair market value can be used if desired. Generally the problem with owners "acting up" or not working any longer stems from their knowledge of their secure ownership position with their shares legally in their possession forever. Too much job security can make some employees very bold and nonproductive, as anyone who has had to deal with civil service personnel or tenured professors can testify.

If you have concluded by this time that I strongly advise against passing out ownership shares in your venture too early or to too many individuals, you are absolutely correct. The traffic cop told the backseat driver, "One driver to a car, please." In military terms, "One captain to each ship." In the small business, "One boss at a time." You cannot run your small business by committee, discussion or consensus during the early years. There is not time for committee meetings or joint discussions. Someone, and I repeat *one*, must be in charge. Big corporations or governments must rule by shared authority and responsibility. They have the size and staying power to survive mistakes, wars, upheavals, and delays, but the small venture cannot wait. The fleeting opportunity presents itself now. Immediate action and decision is required right now or you will lose the opportunity. Someone has to say "yes" or "no," "do it" or "let it pass." If, at this stage, the owner/officers have to meet, discuss, argue, and then decide, it makes it even more difficult to survive and grow. I have never heard any successful small business persons later say they could have done better if they had distributed some of their stock earlier to other people. Yet I have heard them moan over the mistakes they made in awarding ownership stock to others who, for whatever reason, did not measure up or perform well enough to justify their ownership position.

Remember, mistakes made in your bylaws or in who owns what part of your new venture are difficult or even impossible to correct later. These are big mistakes that are not apparent at the time, but slowly become more evident and more difficult to handle as time goes on. Look at the way the big, successful corporations handle their stock options. Generally they are reserved for a very few highly placed individuals. They are given a target to reach in future sales, profit, or return on investment. Their success must be due to their efforts. If they reach it, they get the stock option; if they fail, they do not. This way you don't give out in advance valuable stock. You can't lose, only gain. People at lower levels receive cash bonuses, raises, promotions, or company cars for their efforts. Not a bad system, is it? If it works for big corporations why can't it work, in exactly the same way, for you?

Hold onto your stock for as long as you can. Be generous with anything else, but be a miser with your company stock. You never know the effect it can have on the recipient, on you, or on your small business. Unless you plan buy/sell arrangements, you cannot ever be sure you will even see the stock again. It can end up in the hands of people who have no interest in you or your company at all.

Internal bickering has led to the downfall of many successful, growing enterprises. It is human nature, I guess. As said earlier, I have never seen or heard about any fights or arguments at a funeral. Everyone is on their best behavior, and, in their mutual sorrow, compassion rises. Relatives and former friends, with whom you had some difficulty in the past, shake hands, kiss, and hug each other. The former good relationship is restored, only someone, whom they both loved, had to die for it to happen. Now, at a wedding, which is supposed to be a very happy and joyous occasion for all of the guests, what do we find? I have seen fights, insults, and even open hostility demonstrated.

I recently read in the newspapers about a riot at a wedding reception where the police had to intervene. I have never seen or heard of fighting as a company goes into bankruptcy, which is the corporate equivalent of a funeral and burial. Everyone is so quiet, kind, and compassionate, but it does no good. It is too late, the corporate body is dead. Again, when times are good and the company is prospering, I have seen some pretty rough stuff. I do not attend company Christmas parties anymore. I have seen such bizarre behavior that resulted in open hostility and even dismissal from the company due to things said while "celebrating" the company's good fortune. These company parties are the equivalent of wedding receptions. Do you see similar behavior? I cannot for the life of me figure out why some people behave this way, but they do. If one of these people is also a part owner in your enterprise, you have a big problem and you cannot correct it.

If you don't like me and never did, I am sorry, so come and say it at my funeral, it won't bother me at all, but please don't do it at the reception when I am receiving the Small Businessman of the Year award. All that does is needlessly detract from one happy day. Don't bicker and argue over trivia when the company is prospering. It is pointless and only detracts from the overall contentment of business success which may be only temporary. Owners tend to bicker, that's human nature. The best way to keep arguing to an absolute minimum is to keep the number of owners in your enterprise to an absolute minimum, until, of course, the day you go public. That is an entirely different matter.

AVOID NEPOTISM

One final caveat about ownership in the small business. Do not go into business with relatives or friends. Having close, personal relationships among co-owners just adds to the many problems and difficulties that any new and growing company has to solve. The close friend or worse the family member can compound the whole situation and make it worse. Your business or the relationship may survive, but not both. I tried it and the business survived, but we are no longer friends, just business associates. Others whom I know lost both. So do business at the office and meet your friends and relatives at home after working hours. A very successful and very nice businessman I know says this constantly, "I have no friends at work, only business associates. I have my friends and loved ones at home." Mix them up at your peril!

4

STRUCTURAL AND LEGAL MISTAKES YOU MUST AVOID

AFTER PLANNING, the next step in the management function is organization. You set up the structure to implement your plan. Any plan, no matter how wonderful, is just a piece of paper unless someone later carries out the plan. You need an organization for this purpose. With one eye on the plan, you must create a structure of people and areas of responsibility that can turn the plan into reality. What is the biggest mistake to make? Simple! You have no organization at all. The new business entrepreneur just goes in every day and personally directs everyone all day long. Well, in that case, you really do have an organization, I suppose, and it has two levels. The owner, you, is at one level, and everyone else is one level down. Don't consider this as a rare or unusual situation. It is all too common in many small outfits. As previously mentioned, I knew of an owner who personally tried to handle 100 people all at the same level, reporting directly to him. This is the most extreme case I have ever seen, but two levels of organization is not all that unusual in the small venture.

CHANGE IS THE NAME OF THE GAME

A new venture operates in a very dynamic situation. Sales can double or be cut in half in a matter of days. A new job or the loss of your one major contract can rearrange or eliminate your priorities in very short order. All of this makes it very, very difficult to organize anything well. Even very large companies for whom I have worked would reorganize and change the structure quite frequently. At least twice a year or so, we would see new "org charts" posted on the bulletin boards. Our desks were moved so often we suggested they should be on wheels. It was all very disturbing.

I well remember at a former place of employment going to work one Monday morning and finding my office empty of all furniture and the same for all of the people in my department. We had been reorganized and moved over the weekend to a new building, and we knew nothing about it at the time. When I saw my boss and inquired about my empty office, he replied, "Maybe we are trying to tell you something, Bill."

Organizational mistakes, in general, are not as serious as planning or ownership mistakes because if your plan is basically sound, and you have no ownership problems, you will have the staying power to reorganize and correct organizational errors. I am not by any means saying that mistakes in organizing the job cannot be serious or even fatal, because they can be if unrecognized or if left uncorrected. Errors in planning can manifest themselves later at the organizational level, and it is well to know where the problems lie. If not, you will spend time trying to correct the effect of your problem, not the basic cause. That is like giving a shot of painkiller to a person with a broken leg. The pain goes away temporarily, but returns later because the real problem was not identified.

What are some organizational mistakes?

1. No organization at all
2. Too much organization
3. The rigid organization
4. Too many changes in organization
5. Organizing around special people
6. Organizing in name only

ORGANIZE QUICKLY

As was said earlier, "the worst plan is no plan." Also, the worst organization is no organization. However, a very small outfit can function with no organization as long as it stays small and plans to remain small. One boss gives all of the orders. Also, this boss had better be very healthy and not ever out sick. If he or she dies, that demise would coincide with the death of your enterprise as well. Corporations are supposed to be immortal, but not if they are one-man shows. Owners running one-man shows certainly are important, like the star athlete on any team. Their presence or absence from the field means the difference between victory or defeat. This may make the "star" feel good, but in such cases, you do not have a team or a corporation, you have a star plus various supporting players who cannot function without the star. Is that what you want your company to be? If you are the star, you work 60–80 hours a week and cannot even take a few days off to go to the beach. If someone else is your star, then you are in for trouble. He or she soon realizes his or her importance to you and your company; you had better be prepared to reward him or her accordingly right away or else he or she may pull out on you or threaten you, which is just as bad.

A friend had a six-man company going. He let one of his employees take a lead role on his first contract to free himself to look ahead for new business. In the middle of his first contract, this employee and another worker came to the boss and demanded a percent of ownership or they would quit. They were key to the success of his first job. He refused this attempt at "blackmail." They walked out and he went out of business on his first job. Just a little mistake of improper organization, that's all, and that was all for him.

When we moved into our current offices several years ago, the owner of the building told me our predecessor had been a very prosperous and growing metals company. Everything was going well until the owner suddenly died. He ran everything and had no organization set up to function without him. His wife and several managers tried to take over and keep it going, but it did not last six months. The company went into bankruptcy, so you can see mistakes in your organization can be as fatal as any other kind of mistake.

You should have an organization and reporting structure from day one so you can quickly supervise, direct, and control the action to catch any problems early on. A 15- to 30-minute meeting late in the day, each day, can keep you up to date if you want to do it. At first, it is necessary, believe me.

MODERATION IN ALL THINGS

Too much organization with too many levels of authority is a bad idea too. Generally this happens when owners try to imitate a larger company's organization because they are familiar with it, since they had previously worked there. Your place is new, it is different, and your plan should not be the same as other companys' plans. Blind imitation is pointless, in fact it is even destructive. In general, it is better at first to under- rather than to over-organize. If you have any doubt at all about setting up another level of authority, don't do it. When you find later that you don't need it, you will find others will resist and resent being removed from the "org chart" as a supervisor, manager, or whatever. There may be no change in salary, but loss of the prestige is considered a demotion.

I have seen good people quit their jobs over a change in their job titles. I lost an excellent secretary some years ago because I reorganized the office staff and she resented being reassigned to report to another senior secretary whom she considered junior to her. They had previously all taken direction directly from me; but the staff grew to five secretaries. I wanted to deal with one and let her direct the others. How much worse would it have been if I had removed someone from a higher level and eliminated the position as unnecessary? Organize from the top down by plan, and not from the bottom up, as I did in this situation. A good span of control is about one to five. For every five people, have a supervisor. For every five supervisors, have a manager and so on. This means the previously mentioned 100-man outfit could have three management or supervisory levels: the boss and four managers, each with five supervisors of five others. The multi-level 20-man outfit could function with two levels as well. The five to one ratio can vary in some cases that are temporary up to even ten workers to one supervisor. Beyond that, there are too many employees for one person to direct and control properly.

RIGID THINGS SUDDENLY BREAK

The rigid organization does not change no matter what happens. Big bureaucracies are like that. They don't have to change so they won't. I left government service in Washington, DC in 1958. Twenty years later, I was in town on business and went over to visit my former associates who were still there. I entered the old office and twenty years rolled away quickly. My old desk was still there and my old chair, too. I sat down in the chair and the left arm fell off, as it did when I was there. I asked why wasn't it fixed. They laughed and said the "work order" was still waiting its turn. The same "org chart," same job categories, and same people in most cases were there; few promotions and few transfers had occurred. It was as if I had never left.

A rigid organization has no place in the small business world where change is the name of the game. A big new job can require an entirely new setup which must be implemented quickly, or else. Consider your basic plan as something to change slowly, but don't be afraid to reorganize quickly when you think it must be done. You can always change it back if you must. These mistakes are correctable, even if people get upset. They will calm down in a week or so, so don't be afraid to experiment with the organization until you zero in on the best one. But please be cautious about setting up too many levels. As said earlier, experience indicates people can become permanently upset by loss of a job title once awarded. You can always create new levels, but it is difficult to take them away.

Many entrepreneurs have strong personalities and that is what drives them to start a business with the fixed idea that they can succeed. That is great, so long as they are right. The difference between being steadfast and being stubborn is you are steadfast when you are right. With strong personalities or "outsized egos" this attitude carries over into other areas. There may be a tendency for the owner who starts up a new venture to set up a rigid or fixed organizational structure and stick with it, come "hell or high water." If later they were proven right, they can point with pride to "sticking to their guns" when everyone else

STRUCTURAL AND LEGAL MISTAKES YOU MUST AVOID

said "don't do it." If they fail, they quietly join the casuality list of those who did not make it.

On average though, it is best not to be rigid. Things that are rigid and cannot bend or adjust tend to suddenly snap and break. The small business is dynamic and must be quick to respond to changing circumstances in order to seize the opportunity when it flies by. This is one of the greatest advantages the small outfit has over the big bureaucracies. You are a cat, and they are an elephant. If your organizational structure is small but rigid, you are a cat who moves like an elephant. Such things tend to get stepped on with no one even noticing. Don't give up the greatest asset that the small business has. Be quick! It pays off!

ENOUGH IS ENOUGH

Too many changes in the organization is also a problem. Most people do not like change. A change from the known to the unknown causes much needless concern. Sudden and drastic changes in the organization cause confusion, morale problems, and reduced efficiency. In the small outfit, you can get everyone together and explain what you are doing and why. A company with 100 or fewer employees can do this, but, in so doing, do not give the impression that you are seeking their approval or consent. Think it out and plan it with your managers. Then tell all what the new organization is for, why you are implementing it, and what you expect from them. You are now explaining the decision, not seeking approval.

Do this with your managers beforehand. Any public display by the boss of uncertainty, ignorance, or confusion really upsets the work force. The top person in any organization, regardless of age, is considered a parent figure, and when anyone sees dad or mom showing fear or confusion the effect upon the group can be shattering. Frequent changes in the organization can be construed by some as confusion, uncertainty, or a sign of impending disaster. They are not too far off the mark because, from my experience, sudden or frequent changes in the organization did result from problems rather than responses to new opportunities. In the small business, things can change quickly, and if, as a result, you must alter your organization, by all means do so, and do it quickly, but keep it within reasonable bounds. Let everyone know it is due to new clients, increased sales, or bigger staff. These are good and valid reasons for sudden change.

Another point about organization changes should be mentioned here. If your clients are big organizations, like the government, it is a good idea to explain to the client's representative what you are doing. Here is why. Since they work in a bureaucracy that may change little, they may be conditioned to view any organizational change anywhere as bad per se. Something must be wrong with you and your new outfit, otherwise, why so many changes? If you look for and expect new contracts from this big client, do not make the mistake I saw a colleague make. When asked by his client why he reorganized so often, he said his internal company operations were no one's business but his own. He said all the client should be concerned with is the product or service to be delivered and the price and schedule for delivery, not how he chose to organize his company to get the job done. He was correct in theory, but as a result, the client's representative advised his bosses that the small company was "unstable." A new opportunity for an even bigger contract arose and my friend's outfit was not considered because the client considered the company to be poorly managed. Some view stability and consistency as a sign of a solid, conservative, and efficient outfit, especially in legal and accounting areas. Please keep this in mind. Many act on how they perceive a situation to be without taking the time to find out the true situation.

DON'T SET UP INDISPENSABLE PEOPLE

Organizing around special people is a touchy situation. If you ever do it, you should make it clear it is a temporary situation and the special organization has a definite end date. Proposal

STRUCTURAL AND LEGAL MISTAKES YOU MUST AVOID 53

teams, special projects, or a team set up to repair a situation that has gone wrong or to handle some emergency situation are what I mean. In these cases, using the special and unique talents of individuals for a limited period of time (three to six months or so) is necessary and good. However, if you set up a permanent organization geared and tailored specifically to any individual, you may end up in a worse situation than before.

A good organization should be able to stay in place regardless of who comes and goes, with little overall change in the level of performance. Look at the military. One general comes in to replace another. If the division does not perform as well under the new general, he or she is replaced. They do not reorganize the division structure. Time has proven the efficiency of the organization structure through years of trial and error. If you set up a permanent organization around Joe or Mary and only they can make it work, you are setting up a "key man/woman" situation. What if they get sick, die, or resign to go elsewhere?

Sometimes in a new outfit, you have no choice and people do get into key situations. You can take some precautions. Let me explain by example. Several years ago we got a job with a client on the West Coast, and I had to send one manager and five others to work and live 3,000 miles away from the home office. The new manager was the key man. If anything happened to him during the period of performance (which was five years), we would have had a serious problem. We made a work contract with him so he would not leave for the period of performance. Also, we took out a key-man term life insurance policy on him for the same period. These policies are not that expensive since the odds highly favor his survival. These precautions are well worth the small price to pay, because one such problem early on can cause you great difficulty. If Mary and Joe leave you by choice or by some power beyond anyone's control, they are gone. You and your company remain to pick up the pieces and try to go on.

If your organization can stay as is, and you simply replace Mary or Joe, you give some stability and staying power to your outfit. Sure, each of us ends up doing things our own special way, but within the bounds of the organization structure, I hope. Any changes in the organization due to the presence or absence of any person or a few people shows that the structure is fragile and too easily subject to disruption.

Also, it is not to your personal advantage to do this. If you have a 50 or 75 person outfit organized into three projects, and each project leader is key and difficult to replace, what would you do if all three together realized this and came to you to demand special consideration? Your organization set them up in key situations. You cannot replace them without serious disruption to your enterprise. Now what do you do? This sort of thing has happened. I know individuals who barely survived and some did not survive situations like this due to an organizational mistake. It will never happen if people know they are not key or vital to your organization. Important yes, but not key.

THE SHADOW ORGANIZATION

Organizing in name only occurs when the organizational structure does not truly reflect the power structure. This can happen even in big outfits where the "org charts" show the names of those who are in nominal charge, but in day-to-day operations are not really in charge at all. Some Machiavellian manipulator, working behind the scenes, is the power behind the throne, and really runs things. When we discover to whom we must go to get decisions and things done, then the "org chart" is a useless piece of paper. In fact, it is worse than useless, it is actually wrong. I would rather have no paper or a blank piece of paper then have a paper with erroneous or misleading information on it, wouldn't you?

Any organization that assigns responsibility without giving authority is bad for the individual concerned and the organization as well. In the small business, with the owners or owner present, an organization in name only can easily develop. Some problem or difficulty arises and the managers head right to the owner. If he or she directly intervenes and countermands the subordinate manager's instructions, you now have a useless organization. It functions normally, but when real problems arise the intermediate levels are ignored at both ends. Certainly you, as the owner of a small outfit, want to be advised by your subordinates if they think anything is going wrong. Do not shut your door to them. You want the information; however, you should handle it via your organization, because if you don't, your managers won't manage.

If you try to resolve your problems via your managers but the problems persist, you just found out you have poor managers. Your organization structure is sound, you just have to replace a poor manager. A well-organized and good reporting structure will uncover and identify "problem people" very quickly. A poorly organized place or one with no organization has the same problem, but is unable to either identify it or know what caused it. A good employee, who gets conflicting instructions or no direction due to a poor organization, does not perform well. A poor employee also performs poorly. How do you know the real reason?

Telling an owner to let managers fix their own mistakes is easier said than done. Since it is your baby, the natural tendency is to jump right in, take over, and do it your way. Please don't unless it is absolutely necessary. You will destroy the organization, because your managers will be afraid to make decisions. It is a question of your good judgment. If you possibly can, let the managers run their own shows. There have been times when I would become aware of a situation or problem and I thought I knew exactly what to do. If I found myself thinking about going into the meeting, grabbing a piece of chalk, and barking out orders, I would quickly go home, take a shower, have a good dinner, go to bed, and come back the next day and ask the manager what happened. In almost all such cases, the manager figured out what to do, and in a number of situations his or her solution was better than what I had planned to do.

Generally new outfits are poorly organized at first. It behooves you to organize as quickly as you can, so you don't have to do it all yourself. I know it is very difficult to allow subordinate managers to do their thing, and make mistakes at your expense so they can learn and grow. You want to rush in and put things "right" your way. Fine, but it limits your opportunity to expand and grow. No matter how good you are, you are only one person. On the other hand, complete delegation and isolation in which you let them completely do it their way can put you out of business before you know what hit you. They apologize, go work elsewhere, and leave you to the bankruptcy courts with a dead corporation to bury. Like anything else, it is a question of judgment on your part and timing.

The jobs you have and circumstances will all affect how you organize. At least they should. There is no "right" way, but there are lots of wrong ways, some of which have just been presented. In the final analysis, use what works for you. After all, that is why you started the new venture, isn't it? You wanted to do it your way, but you don't have to repeat other people's mistakes as you "zero in" on the best organizational structure for you. I can't attempt to tell you how to organize, no one can. You may come up with an entirely new method that works great for you. Others notice your success and try to imitate you but fall flat on their face, because they are not you or circumstances changed. There is no master plan on how to organize your place, except the one you develop. Mistakes made here can usually be repaired unless left unattended. Organizational mistakes are not, in themselves, all as serious or as permanent as planning or ownership mistakes. So, if you have to make mistakes, make them here, not in the other areas in which you don't get a second chance.

LEGAL PROBLEMS

Let's now proceed into legal mistakes, some of which can be corrected and some that cannot. Mostly legal errors are correctable (except mistakes in your bylaws), but they cost you needless time, effort, expense, and aggravation, and divert you from your real task of making your outfit survive and grow. Some can be fatal, though. No one gains anything by going to court as a defendant. The best you can hope for is being found

STRUCTURAL AND LEGAL MISTAKES YOU MUST AVOID

innocent and you lose your lawyer's fees and all the time, effort, and worry in preparing your defense. Hardly a good expenditure of time and money, is it?

Selecting a good lawyer to be your corporate counsel is very important. There are all kinds of lawyers, so get one who knows about small businesses. There are many typical legal situations in which small businesses tend to find themselves, just as there are typical situations in which big companies can get involved. You want a small business lawyer, not your brother-in-law or the old family friend and advisor. You get what you pay for, so get the best. A poor or inexperienced lawyer can lead you into trouble and just as doctors bury their mistakes, lawyers' mistakes end up in court. The lawyer is never the defendant, you are.

YOU AREN'T AS FREE AS YOU THINK

You may think (and hope) that in running your own venture, you can do exactly what you want for the first time in your life in operating your own company. This is not true! At the beginning, or until you are big enough to afford others to work for you, you are your own personnel department, technical director, salesperson, and complaints department. You hire, fire, promote, and transfer as you think best; however you had better do it all legally and in all likelihood you are not fully experienced in all of these areas of special knowledge. You don't know what you don't know, but ignorance of the law is no excuse.

Even little things creep in and can bother you. For example, before I started my outfit, I had been in middle management for about 15 years. I always had a secretary, full time. Upon starting my new outfit, I could only afford a part-time secretary for about a year. I was making my own business calls and I found I was dialing many wrong numbers. It got so bad, I went to the doctors to have my eyes checked. It was not my eyes. I had not dialed the telephone in so many years, I had forgotten how to dial correctly. How dumb can you get? Here is a 40-year old man, who is running a growing business, who cannot do what a five-year-old can do. I could design orbits around the moon, but I had difficulty with a telephone. This is an example of the "little" things you have to do for yourself when you start to run your own outfit. I also emptied wastebaskets and cleaned the office floor on Saturdays. We could not afford a cleaning service at the start. I still shovel the snow off the office steps when I arrive early (it is a habit I can't shake) on snowy days so no one will slip and fall on the way in. So strong ego or not, don't be reluctant to do what has to be done.

POLICIES AND PROCEDURES

Prepare a book of company policies and procedures. Don't wait, as I did, for each situation to arise before writing a company policy on the subject. In this case, you may want to imitate the big companies. If you have a set of policies and procedures where you worked before, look at every single subject and decide which may possibly apply in your situation, and prepare a policy on the subject. As you hire people, on day one, they read the policies and procedures manual and sign a statement that they will abide by all company policies and procedures. All big outfits do this. It is well for you to start out with one so you won't get into legal hassles needlessly.

For example, we are a software service company. As we started to grow, we hired good people to work on big software projects at our client's facilities. The client got to know our people and offered the best ones better positions on their staff. After losing seven good people in a few years' time (I got smart slowly), we prepared a work agreement in our policies and procedures manual. It stated that no employee of our company would solicit or accept offers of employment from our clients until one year after they left our employment. That stopped it entirely, except a funny thing happened when we asked all current employees to sign it. Two refused and one of them was a senior manager. The employee left and the manager was persuaded to sign it by our company lawyer. What did they have in mind? I think I know, don't you?

Prepare a policies and procedures manual right at the start and avoid any possible legal hassles. Sooner or later you will have to dismiss someone. You had better learn how to do it legally or stand by for trouble later. It must be done correctly with a written legal procedure or else. People have gone to court over the right to wear beards, dress code violations, and other minor issues. These needless hassles can all be avoided if you write down your policies and everyone agrees to work by them. When you invoke them, you won't get feedback.

You cannot hire, fire, promote, transfer, discipline, demote, or take just about any action at work based on age, sex, national origin, race, or religion. You had better know what the laws are and keep them up to date. Consider this situation. You finish one job and get a new contract. It is for a military project. You start to transfer the staff to the new job. Someone tells you she doesn't want to work on a military job. It is against her conscience. You have no other job for her as the current job draws to a close. Can you dismiss her? If so, are is she entitled to unemployment compensation at your company's expense? You had better know! It is a little known fact that unemployment compensation insurance is paid 100 percent by the employer. Not one cent is paid by the employee or the government. If any of your employees draw unemployment insurance, you have to replace the funds by a higher payment rate the next year. How would you like to dismiss an employee for cause who rushes down to claim unemployment insurance? You have no written records or procedures to prove he or she was released for nonperformance or for valid cause. In such cases, the fired employee will be awarded the weekly checks at your expense, just because you kept no written records to prove to the claims adjuster that you had a valid reason. I learned this the hard way. It is not deadly, just expensive.

PAPER, PAPER EVERYWHERE

There are a myriad of forms you must fill out and send to various government agencies. The paperwork blizzard is blinding and you must do it correctly. Again, errors may not be fatal, but they are bothersome and take your time. A good CPA consulting firm is well worth the expense, because if you try (as we did at first) to do it ourselves, we made the mistake of not knowing what to do. You have such things as:

1. Social Security
2. Federal Unemployment Expense
3. State Unemployment Expense
4. Workers' Compensation
5. IRS
6. State Tax Department
7. Company Insurance
8. Employee Insurance
9. Company Owner's Legal Expenses
10. Buy/Sell Agreements

and many others as well. A legal oversight or mistake in one area can stop you cold. Do you know that, in some states, it is a criminal, not a civil, offense to miss a payroll? If, for any reason, you should, do you want to be arrested by just one unhappy employee? It can and has happened. Don't let it happen to you. Who needs it?

ACCOUNTING PROBLEMS

Are you going to use a cash or accrual accounting system? Do you know the difference? You'd better! The cash system operates on the basis of cash flow only. If you work on a job for four months and get paid $40,000 at the end, then you have no income on your books for three months and $40,000 income in the fourth. The accrual system applies the $40,000 across the four months at $10,000 per month as you accrued the expenses and profit as you did the job. This is much more businesslike and truly reflects the way your company operates. Big outfits use the accrual system. Great! There is only one problem, you have no money, just accrued income and profit, in your ac-

STRUCTURAL AND LEGAL MISTAKES YOU MUST AVOID 61

counts receivable. If your fiscal year ends before you are paid, and your accrual system lists accrued profit for work done, you owe the IRS the taxes on the "profit" whether or not you have been paid.

We started out with the accrual system and found ourselves borrowing to pay the IRS the taxes due on "profit" from government contracts for which we had not been paid. Sometimes the client is very slow in paying you. I asked our lawyer, "Why can't we send in our IRS tax form, and list the amount due us from the government, and tell the IRS to get what we owe them from the other government agency who owed us for more than we owed the IRS?" My lawyer said, "Sure, Bill, try it and I will get rich defending you in tax court and you will lose." So, your choice of the legal accounting system you wish to use is important. You can change from one to the other later, but, if you do, the IRS might just drop in to find out why. Think ahead a bit. Maybe use the cash system for a year or two, then you can adopt the nice efficient accrual system just like the big corporations. Using the wrong system too early can cost you needless borrowing and interest expenses that could well have been avoided if only you knew. A good CPA and legal advisor should be able to advise you, based on your own individual situation. I cannot recommend either system to the readers of this book, so I won't try. Get all the information you can, then decide for yourself.

KNOW WHAT YOU ARE DOING

If you start a new outfit, I assume you are planning for it to grow and survive, so make sure you look into all of these "little legal" situations that will arise along the way. Most, as said earlier, are just bothersome, but some can be expensive, and a few can be fatal. In any case, you really don't need any of them and most can be taken care of by some forethought and planning on your part. Use your legal and CPA advisors, but do not let them make any decisions for you. Make them explain the situation to you, list the alternatives (i.e., cash versus accrual system), make their recommendations, and then you decide what to do. After all, it is your outfit.

Our first attorney picked our fiscal year to end at a time when his law office was not busy. Later we had to change it to suit our individual needs. Our CPA, on his own, set up a straight line depreciation policy for our capital equipment. We later changed it to accelerated depreciation to gain more cash for our growing company up front, when we needed it. The CPA thought straight line was neater, and we did not even know one from the other. When we asked him to explain the various depreciation methods that were legally available, we quickly chose another method that was much better for our needs. It all adds up. A few hundred here and a few thousand there.

At the start, almost all of us are cash short, and we don't want to or just can't afford the legal and CPA services that any growing company really requires. I have never heard of any small business person complain of expensive but good legal and CPA services, but have I ever heard horror stories from those who tried to do it all for themselves to save a "buck" and it ended up costing them thousands later. Would you treat yourself or give yourself a physical exam because you don't want to pay for a good doctor to do it for you? I hope you wouldn't. Would you pay a doctor to diagnose your illness and then not take the medicine he or she prescribes for you? I hope you wouldn't, but I know some people who do just that.

The corporate body has many similarities to the human body. It is a legal entity just as you are. It has high infant mortality just as human babies do. It has teenage problems in which some cannot grow up. It has old age problems too, in which corporate senility sets in and kills it off. Refusing to seek or follow proper legal and CPA advice is a mistake, and I have made my share. Don't you do it. As I look back on the things I didn't do that I should have known about and should have taken care of, I know there must be a big corporate guardian angel up there somewhere to guide us through our ignorance and early follies and mistakes. I made about every mistake I discussed and

STRUCTURAL AND LEGAL MISTAKES YOU MUST AVOID

some I am too embarrassed to even mention now. If you only knew, you would conclude that I am so dumb this book wouldn't be worth reading. It was a question of what the old SBA fellow told me. It wasn't that I did not know the answers or how to get them, it was worse; I didn't even know the questions.

SEEK INFORMATION

In these areas of organization and legal situations, go talk to other small business people. As long as you are not going to be in direct competition with them, you will find that many will be only too glad to advise you, mostly about mistakes they made due to being naive or ignorant of such matters and what difficulty it caused for them. They can recommend or not recommend legal and CPA advisors for you to consider. You can learn from our mistakes or go out and do them all over again and learn by your own experience. The choice of course is yours, as it should be.

In the areas of legal and CPA activities, the more formal and organized you are, the better. Many will judge the maturity and efficiency of your company by the image you project to the outside world; i.e., new clients, banks, government agencies, or people you want to hire. Planning and ownership are mainly internal matters and do not show directly to the outside. Only the effects of these things show via on-time delivery, low price, no overruns, and satisfied clients. This is all great stuff, as you slowly and steadily build a reputation with your current clients. Your organization and your legal situation (good or bad) show themselves directly to the outside world and can quickly affect your reputation for good or ill. If the word goes around that your new company is having or has had some legal problems or the organization is weak and turnover is too high and morale is low, you cannot gain anything from this. It can hurt you in many ways, precisely because you cannot directly confront or correct these stories whether or not they are based on fact. The harm is done.

DISCIPLINE PAYS OFF

We got our first big opportunity to direct our own staff on a government contract some years ago, rather than having to work on site at the government facilities, under the watchful eye of government technical supervisors. Our organization and our correct reputation that we are a no-nonsense outfit helped us gain this contract. Everyone had to be at their desks on time each day, and the managers kept close reins on the work and schedules and budget. We show our clients an organization that satisfies them that we are capable of directing and controlling the job. We organize by projects or clients and, today, the "org chart" is substantially the same as it has been for years. The clients and projects have changed, and we have several more projects. We based our organization from our experience in the government, and from working at large commercial organizations. These big places have had years of experience with various organizational methods, so you can learn from them, but don't blindly copy them. Use them as a point of departure and adjust and "tweak" the "org chart" to your own special goals, needs, and interests. If your "org charts" end up similar but not identical to the way the big companies do it, you won't be too far off the mark. However, if you have something that is entirely different, i.e., one boss with 100 subordinates or a seven-level hierarchy to manage 20 people, look again. You may well find what you are doing is not the best or even an efficient method, and sooner or later, it will catch up to you. In the small outfit, it is generally sooner.

As for legal problems, we had our share of minor scrapes due to lack of proper attention and preplanning on my part. In my naiveté, twice I prepaid for services and supplies which were not delivered and two court actions resulted. We "won" and the funds due to us were returned, but, when considering the time and effort on my part that was taken away from attention to growth and sales and the legal fees involved, it just was not worth it. The best way to avoid legal difficulties is planning, and close work with your lawyer and CPA. It is like fire prevention. If you do it well, nothing happens and that is exactly what you want. Any company, sooner or later, will get into some legal hassle for one reason or another, but it is best to put them off for as long as possible. When one shows up, you have a good organization to show, and a legal, written audit trail to follow which explains and justifies your actions.

5

STEERING CLEAR OF FINANCIAL PITFALLS

YOU MUST MAKE A PROFIT

THIS CHAPTER IS written on the assumption that your basic reason for starting a new venture is to make a profit, make your company grow and later become an "instant millionaire" by either going public or selling your nice, growing company to a big outfit who wants your company's capability, your clients, or your fine staff and organization to blend into their big corporate plan. I mention this now because a number of people start new ventures for other reasons. They do not want to grow. They want to stay small and they want freedom and time to do other things. The new venture is merely a vehicle to run so they can pursue other interests in their own way. In any case, though, whatever your reason is for operating your small outfit and whatever you choose to do with the income earned, you still have to make some sort of profit or at least be able to pay yourself some salary and not go into debt.

The Small Business Administration (SBA) in Washington, DC recently established a hot line for information or advice from those interested in starting or operating a small business. The *Wall Street Journal* (27 December 1982, p. 11) reports that the majority of callers ask about how to get money to do what they want to do. So, it can be seen that whatever your plans may be, and no matter how well you are organized, "money is the name of the game" in the small (or big) business venture. You need it to survive and grow.

The corporate body and the human body have a number of similarities. A company that is losing money is bleeding to death and sooner or later will topple over from running out of funds. This is not the cause of their demise, it is the effect of another cause somewhere else in the operation. Let's assume that you are running at a profit. Great! You are off and running. Now what can happen to cause you difficulty under such circumstances? Plenty!

NO RECORDS—NO KNOWLEDGE

In a business, the way you keep score is by first getting sales, then subtracting expenses from the sales, and the remainder is profit. Sounds simple enough, but statistics indicate that over 85 percent of small business owners do not know how to read and understand a Profit and Loss statement or a balance sheet. If you are trying to operate a small outfit and you don't know how to keep score, you are in for trouble. Would you play tennis, golf, or football and let someone else (your opponent, perhaps?) keep score for both of you? Hardly! Then it is not a good idea to try to operate a business without knowing the rules of the game and how one keeps score or whether one is winning or losing.

In business, it is simple. You are winning when you are making a profit, and you are losing when you are not. However, what if you can't tell the difference? I have seen this happen, even in a very big company. At a former place of employment, the engineering department built three new devices as part of an R&D project. The new devices worked and the client wanted to purchase ten more with options for many to follow. The company was unable to come up with a price for the devices due to improper record keeping by the department doing the R&D project. Poor and/or nonexistent time and financial records made it impossible to go back and figure out the costs for one unit.

Most new small companies keep very poor records until something like this creeps up or crashes down on them. If they survive, then they learn the value of keeping financial records from the first day. So in addition to your business plan, as discussed in Chapter 2, you have to prepare a financial plan to implement your business plan. If you don't you will run out of funds. You had better personally do this. If you delegate financial planning to others, you may rue the day. I did it personally for 14 years and then decided it was time to let someone else do it for me. On our next contract there was a $300,000 overrun, followed by a $270,000 underrun on the one after that, so I am back into the financial picture again. Everyone was too busy trying to do a perfect technical job, so they did not pay any attention to their costs or schedule. Keep your hand firmly on your costs and profit figures and jump quickly when they depart from your monthly or weekly financial plan.

What are some typical financial mistakes?

1. You start out undercapitalized.
2. You cannot keep track of costs.
3. You confuse growth with profit.
4. Bad debts catch you unprepared.
5. You "live it up" too soon.
6. You ignore the business cycle.

WITHOUT FUNDS YOU CAN'T DO ANYTHING

Almost all small new ventures are undercapitalized at the start. Few people will ever advance you money and not expect prompt and complete repayment with interest. Before you start, you should complete your financial plan to match your business plan and have on hand sufficient funds to keep you going to match your business plan. In addition to start-up funds, you must consider your working capital requirements, or enough cash to keep you going for a couple of months. Here is why. Typically a new venture performs some services or produces a product and then waits for payment. If you mass produce some item and put it in inventory, it is a corporate asset and looks great on the balance sheet, but you still have to sell it.

Let's assume that you are in the fortunate position of selling your product or service as fast as you can make it. Great! Now you wait 30 to 60 or even 90 days for payment. During this same period, you have expenses that must be paid, such as employees' salaries. We have already discussed what can happen to you if you miss a payroll. In addition, you find that most of the things you must purchase must be paid in advance. Such things as rent, insurance, supplies, and materials call for cash up front. Suppliers know you are a new venture with no credit rating as yet and they know the small business failure rate as well as you do, so you pay COD. Insurance and rent will always require advance payments. That is the way they operate.

So your working capital requirements for two or three months for a going small outfit can be quite large. If you do not have capital available at the start, where are you going to get it later on?

Running short of working capital is a very common small business killer during the first year or two. Late payments for your accounts receivables or the sudden loss of an existing contract can end it all too quickly. A word about accounts receivables is in order here. In business, everyone tries to get other people's money (OPM). The trick is to get the money you need from someone else to use as you see fit and pay it back slowly, at as low an interest rate as possible. Before you jump at a job for a big outfit, check out their payment cycle. Some pay promptly, i.e., 30 days or less, but there are some who deliberately wait up to 90 days, so they can retain the cash for that period and use it before they pay anyone. These are called "slow payers" and if your first few jobs are with the slow payers, you may be in for trouble. That is one mistake we did not make, but it was more from chance than anything else, I guess. We had a good financial reserve before we worked for slow payers; I shudder to think what they could have done to us if they had been our only client a few years before. We just would not have survived. We were undercapitalized.

Before you "cut the cord" and jump into your new venture, you had better have your working capital requirements ready at hand, or else. If you get caught short, you will have to, in desperation, sell a major portion of your new venture for a fraction of its potential value. A year or so back, I went to the bank to cash a check. While I was waiting, I overheard a conversation going on at a desk in the lobby. The fellow was very upset and speaking too loudly. He needed $500 to meet his Friday payroll and he was trying to get a short-term loan on Wednesday. The loan officer spoke quietly and the supplicant answered loudly. No, he had no assets. He had already borrowed against his car and furnishings at home. No, it would take too long to get a second mortgage on his home. Would you lend $500 to such a person? I mumbled a silent prayer that it would never happen to me.

Undercapitalization up front can be deadly. I can't tell you how to get the funds you are going to need for your working capital, but you had better figure out what you will need and add a 50 percent Murphy's Law factor for safety before you start out. It can't hurt at all to have too much. Anyone can put on weight or give away their wealth any time they choose, but the opposite is not easy to do. Even if you can, it takes time and, in the small venture, you may run out of time. Being undercapitalized is a chronic problem for many small ventures and increased sales cannot correct it for a long time. In fact, a sudden increase in sales can make an undercapitalized company even worse off, at least temporarily. You need even more cash up front and now your accounts receivables get even larger. Your accounts receivables are real, but you will never collect them because as soon as you get paid (you hope), within 30 days you have another set of monthly invoices to send out. Working capital to finance accounts receivables and other costs are like the bow wave that a ship creates as it glides through the water. The bigger the ship and the faster it goes, the bigger the bow wave becomes, but the ship can never pass through or over it. It is a cost of doing business, so don't be undercapitalized.

LOST IN A JUNGLE OF NUMBERS

You lose track of costs, or worse, you never kept track of them. As stated earlier, 85 percent of small business people can't read or understand the P&L and balance sheets. You can't keep

STEERING CLEAR OF FINANCIAL PITFALLS

score if you don't know how to prepare or read the score card. Accounting is not difficult. It is only arithmetic. You don't have to be a CPA to understand basic accounting. There are even courses in accounting for managers and nonaccounting personnel to teach you how to read and understand basic accounting principles. Do-it-yourself home accounting courses can help. It is better though to take a one-semester course from your local high school extension course or a course at some local college in basic accounting. It is well worth it, believe me. Professional accountants make mistakes too, they are only human. I once caught a $10,000 overpayment due to an arithmetic error our accountant made in making out our IRS tax forms. It was an overpayment, and since I was able to read and follow his calculations, I caught it before we paid too much tax. If you cannot or do not keep track of such things, they will happen to you and you won't even know it. You just start to run short of funds.

Cost accounting or keeping track of your costs is very important. You may be submitting a fixed price for a contract and if you underprice it, you find you are losing money as you do your job, and you don't know why. Overpricing is not too much of a problem. It is very quickly self-correcting. You don't get the job in the first place, because your price is too high. You can't have an accounting problem if you have no sales in the first place. You need something to account for, don't you?

Generally the problem of lack of cost control is a poor organization followed by a poor or no record-keeping system at all. The boss does it all in his or her head or on the back of an envelope, and lets it go with that. If you produce a variety of products, your total profit may be acceptable to you, but do you know precisely how much profit each item you produce earns for you? Some are shocked to learn that their biggest sellers produce the least profit, or, horror of horrors, in some cases, they actually don't make any profit at all; other products that are very profitable are "making up" for the others. I have seen more than one outfit quickly stop producing and selling a particular product and switch to others, when this startling information came to their attention. This has even happened to very large companies, but that is little comfort to the small outfit.

The "biggie" is embarrassed, but survives. You are out of business before you have time to get embarrassed.

GROWTH DOES NOT ALWAYS PRODUCE PROFIT

Confusing growth with profit is another common mistake. That is like confusing activity with action. Activity produces motion and effort. Action produces results and profit. At the start, many judge the success of the small outfit by how many employees you have. People will ask you, "How many people do you have working for you now?" They don't want to ask you how much profit you make. That is too personal, so they ask about employees and then assume that the more employees you have, the more profit you are earning. That is a false assumption. It does not automatically follow that a company employing 500 people is much better off than a 75-person outfit. It is profit that matters. That is what it is all for, isn't it?

When you grow, you need more working capital to fund your monthly cycle and fund your ever increasing accounts receivable. The more business you do and the bigger you become, the greater the amount of money tied up in internal operations. It is always owed to you, but the only way to collect it once and for all is to cease operations, and wait for all bills owed you to be paid. That is no way for any outfit to finally collect all that is due, is it?

Too rapid growth has killed off many a fine small outfit. Your growth and expansion should be in an orderly, planned manner and disordered growth is just as deadly as loss of sales. It just takes a bit longer to catch up with you. When your sales drop off and you have to lay off personnel and borrow to pay your rent or to meet a payroll, you are in immediate trouble and you may not last long. When you borrow to finance a sudden new business opportunity or to start up production for a big new contract, it all looks rosy at first. However if later events prove you were unable to expand fast enough or with sufficient efficiency, your big bank note falls due, you ask for an extension, it is refused, and you stop right there, in the midst of expansion and great activity.

I saw a company go from the startup to $26 million in less than five years and disappear entirely within 30 days for similar reasons. So, growth per se is not always a good thing. Admittedly it is very difficult to refuse a big new job that you truly believe you know how to do; however it is too big for you to swallow at this point in time. You hate to refuse such an opportunity, so you bite the bullet, give it a go, and hope for the best. Some have succeeded, but many more who have tried it have failed. They just could not grow that fast. If you have to borrow at an interest rate that is higher than your percent of profit, you are running up the down escalator. Lots of cash flows through your company. You are hiring and expanding rapidly, everyone sees the activity and growth and thinks you are doing great, yet on the bottom line of your P&L statement, no profit or losses start to accrue.

A decision you have to make early on is what type of clients do you wish to have? Do you want as many customers as possible who each contribute a small amount to your sales, or do you want two or three or one big client upon whom all depends for your survival? Small clients are just as much trouble as big ones, in fact, in many situations, they are even more trouble. You can make more profit, more easily, in dealing with one customer for a $2 million contract than you can with four $500,000 contracts. The natural tendency early on is to go for the big one over the four small ones. Consider what you are doing. You become a slave to this one big client who will soon realize that. Even if you retain the contract, you will find this client almost controlling your company since his or her contract spells life or death for your small outfit. If you grow by tying your company to one or two big contracts, what do you do if either one has to suddenly terminate the business relationship?

Growth and expansion require thought, planning, and additional funds. It is well to stay within your growth plan if you can and progress in an orderly fashion. In modern terms, it is better to slowly launch your rocket and put a small satellite into the business world that stays in orbit rather than launch a big rocket that blasts off, in smoke and flame, rushes to great height, and then quickly returns to earth in an equally spectacular fashion.

COLLECT WHAT'S OWED TO YOU

Bad debts can be deadly to the small venture. A slow-paying client can cause you great difficulty, and one who does not pay at all can put you right out of business. Know whom you are dealing with before you make the deal. If you are dealing with a very large, reputable firm, check their payment cycle (30, 60, or 90 days) and arrange your price accordingly before you sign anything. They will pay you eventually, but it hurts if you have to borrow on your accounts receivables at an interest rate in excess of your profit margin.

Don't be deceived by appearances. The big, flashy, and expensive office does not necessarily mean a successful, profitable, ongoing business. In fact, it may mean exactly the opposite. I know from personal experience, as well as from talking with other business people who were similarly mislead. Check them out with Dun & Bradstreet. Ask for bank or credit references before you let them get in debt to you. If they piously or with arrogance refuse your request, that is an answer in itself, isn't it? Any outfit with a good solid credit rating will only be too happy to have you check on them. In fact, this can be to your advantage. They will respect you for doing business the way they do with their clients. I have requested credit references from very big new clients and was never refused. In fact, I even got a free lunch in Boston at a very expensive private club while we discussed this big outfit's ability to pay us for our services before we started on the job.

In your heady pursuit of new business, you may overlook, to your later sorrow, the fact that you entered into a contract with another company that is in marginal shape and needs the product or service you sell, but wants to use OPM for as long as possible to stave off financial disaster. A spectacular case in the recent past was a company that rose like a rocket and exploded in mid-air. Forty-five million dollars in financing went down the tube and they were still hiring and expanding up to the last moment.

Their demise also killed off a number of small companies that were owed a great deal of money. One was a small rug dealer

STEERING CLEAR OF FINANCIAL PITFALLS

who had sold me rugs for my home. He had a nice, prosperous little business. He accepted an order for 50,000 square yards of rugs for this company's new office building. He ordered the rugs, delivered them, and was not paid. He tried to get his rugs back that were still on the receiving dock and was turned away. The company had filed for bankruptcy and although he could see his rugs in rolls on the floor where he had delivered them, he could not get them back. He went bankrupt too, because he could not pay the rug company, who also had a bad debt. You could say the rug dealer tried to expand too rapidly and paid the price, but financial mistake which causes you to go under doesn't make any difference to you, does it? Also, he could comfort himself by saying the big banks were all taken in too, because they lost millions, but the banks survived and he did not, and that is a very big difference, isn't it?

The rug dealer told me this opportunity for his biggest sale to date was irresistible, so he jumped at it without question. An outfit that big and in such a big new office had to be successful, otherwise why would they order fancy rugs if they were in financial difficulty? The fact was this outfit was in deep financial trouble, because they were spending money they borrowed from the banks. Imagine spending $400,000 or $500,000 of borrowed funds on rugs. No wonder they crashed. If he had checked them out, he would have known they owed everyone in town, but he jumped and tried to expand too quickly and it killed off his little company.

The small outfit does not have the financial reserves or the staying power the big outfits have, so bad debts can be deadly to your growing concern. Even if somehow you go through the courts, and two or three years later you recover a substantial portion of the debt owed you (which you won't), what do you do in the meantime? Know your clients or potential clients well. The company you save may be your own.

YOU CAN ALWAYS SPEND IT LATER

"Living it up" too soon is another financial error in judgment that some small business people make. The time to make hay is while the sun shines. It is not a time to relax or get careless about expenses or costs. Just because your sales and profit are going along well is no reason to increase costs or spend company money because it is there. Yet, this mistake is rather common among growing small businesses.

I am all for enjoying life if you can afford it, but living above one's means is just an accident waiting for a place to happen. It just takes time. Spending and buying things that you really do not need places undue stress on your growing concern. In addition, your top people spend their time and energies arguing for more perks or more assistants than thinking about how to expand the company. I have seen some big arguments over who got what office in the new building, or how much to spend on fancy furniture that was not needed. Your employee's attitude is "Joe got new office furniture, so why can't I get some too?" This sort of thing is very expensive and can be very dangerous in any outfit, especially in the small venture. It also happens in the big outfits. That is why occasionally you will see layoffs in the overhead cost center. Secretaries, staff assistants, support personnel are suddenly let go to lower the overhead to where it belongs. It is difficult to watch those who are let go, but in most cases, they should not have been hired in the first place. Someone went wild with spending cost money because sales were going up.

Why should your overhead and general and accounting expenses increase just because your sales go up? At this point, many acquire or buy things they don't need. Everyone has a need for a telephone on his or her desk. The owners want to enjoy the good life now and take out profit that is needed for later expansion. Times are good, so let's enjoy ourselves.

Some even start to take time off during the work week to make up for countless hours worked earlier to get the small outfit moving and profitable. The same and continued effort at this point could really push the outfit ahead. An athlete can tell you, when you are winning and things are going even better than your game plan, that is the time to press your advantage and pile up a lead so that your opponents can never catch up. It is not a time to relax, take it easy, and rest on your oars. If you do, the lost opportunities do not reoccur when you want or need them later on. Errors of this type strike you right in the corporate pocketbook and affect you financially. You waste or misspend corporate funds because they are available. You are not pressing as hard as you were early on when you did not have the sales base and profit that you have now. It is not a time to relax. It is a time to intensify your efforts because you are winning and gaining corporate strength for even further growth.

For example, two years ago, our telephone bill climbed to over $2,000 per month. I complained about this and was assured they were business calls, yet I saw no new business coming in. Thirty of our staff were transferred to another location to work off site for a new client. Our telephone bill dropped to $700 per month. A year later, they all returned to our home office. I welcomed them back with a memo telling them the telephone bill would not go back up over $700 per month. It has not and we were able to hire a new typist/receptionist with the money saved, produce a new job for someone, and get more typing done, all with no increase in overhead costs.

Letting costs increase just because sales and profits are growing is not a very wise thing to do. It requires your constant attention. It seems to be in the natural order of things for people to spend money simply because there are funds available to be spent. Now, to make matters even worse, if the owners happily participate in this fruitless exercise, they will pay the bill in two ways. First, it is their money that is being misspent right now; later, they will pay again when they need the funds that are gone. Lack of funds prevents them from seizing a new business opportunity.

Build up your cash reserve as quickly as you can. You can always spend it later, with no problem at all. If you decide to go public or to sell out to a bigger company, the more cash you have in your company, the bigger the selling price. Capital gains taxes are much lower than personal income or dividend taxes. Also, companies who want to buy you much prefer to see cash in the company than $1,000,000 worth of supplies, inventory, furniture, or "bricks and iron" that may not be of much value to the acquiring company. Records indicate that an acquiring company always discounts, by a large percentage, the book value you place on your facilities, equipment, desks, furniture, or cars.

However, they won't discount your cash in retained earnings. You are then in the pleasant situation of deciding do you take it all out before the sale or do you leave it in and have the buyer just increase the purchase price directly in proportion to the cash on hand? Think ahead of this probability when the urge to buy things attacks you. Do you really need them or do you just want them because now you can afford it? I have never heard small business persons say that they regret not spending their available funds on office luxuries, new cars, trips, or other nonessentials, but have I ever heard some later complain and moan about spending it too soon and not too wisely. It is your outfit, your life, and your choice, and you win or lose by your own decisions.

THE WORLD AFFECTS YOU WHETHER YOU LIKE IT OR NOT

Ignoring the business cycle is another small business financial error. We have periods of inflation followed by periods of recession. It seems to be in the natural order of things, so if you do not think and plan ahead for when the recession comes, you must pay the price of not surviving. Recent statistics bear this out. *Electronic News* (29 March 1982, p. 1) reports that from 1980 to 1981 bankruptcies increased by 32 percent with small businesses having the lowest survival rate. Even if you don't "live it up" and carelessly waste or misspend your corporate assets when times are good, an economic downturn or some major event, like the oil crisis, can suddenly rise up and crush all before it. In these situations, big companies can survive. They pull in their horns, reduce the level of business expenses, and wait it out. The small company has no staying power and perishes.

SURVIVAL OF THE FITTEST

Indeed, some say this is even desirable. It is called Economic Darwinism, or survival of the fittest. The survivors have shed their "fat," and the marginal outfits have fallen away. The lean and hungry companies who survive quickly jump back into the marketplace as it recovers (as it always does), and these survivors capture all of the business now available with fewer companies competing in the marketplace. I don't particularly like this situation, but you must face it, because it is real, and I believe it will continue to occur, regardless of what our government tries to do to stop it.

Starting a new venture in the midst of an economic downturn is merely putting the odds against your success even higher than the current statistics show. Yet reports say that new incorporations are at an all time high. Unless you plan to produce and sell something that is countercyclical in that sales for the product or service run counter to the economy in general, you are ignoring the big picture which does affect us all whether we like it or not. Years back, we had short-term borrowing from a local bank to meet our monthly cash requirements until we were able to build up sufficient cash reserves. One month our interest rate jumped suddenly. I asked why and was told it was due to Charles de Gaulle who was then president of France. I asked, "What in hell has de Gaulle to do with my company? I don't even know him." The explanation was long and convoluted. De Gaulle was doing something with gold that caused the United States to raise the prime interest rate, which in turn caused the banks to raise all interest rates. I didn't do anything, but macroeconomics had struck us a costly blow. We survived, thank heaven, but if that 3 percent had mattered to us, we would not have stayed in business.

So even though you may concentrate your thoughts and efforts on your new venture, it is well to keep an eye on the macroeconomic business cycle and plan accordingly. What would you do if your current accounts receivables that are promptly paid in 30 days or less suddenly started to stretch out to 60 days or beyond? Could a bad debt suddenly greatly affect you? How much can you tolerate and still survive? If your clients are concentrated in a few big accounts, what would happen if suddenly one or several were cancelled? During any economic downturn, the first things people stop buying are things they don't need, i.e., new cars, clothes, eating out, or vacations. Also, the first things that clients cancel are contracts for outside services or products, before they start to reduce their own work force. This is the correct thing to do. Wouldn't you do the same thing? I would! My own loyal staff comes first, and so does yours or anyone else's, too.

Keep an eye out for the general business cycle, for it can affect you. You have absolutely no control over it. Storms, accidents, and upheavals do occur and the time to prepare is when the sun is shining and the weather is clear. Don't be like the people who say they can't fix the leak in the roof when it is raining and they do not have to fix it when it is not.

SOLVE THE RIGHT PROBLEM

Whatever the reason for any financial mistakes, the result is the same. You run out of funds to keep going. The lack of funds is the effect, not the cause, of your financial problems. It is good to know this because some think the lack of funds is the problem and spend their time trying to acquire the funds. It is not the real problem. A loan or infusion of new funds into any outfit that is cash short, in many cases, is giving a transfusion that merely temporarily keeps them going until they are cash short again. That is why you can't get a bank to give you a loan when you really need it, but you can get one any time you do not need it. It is not a bad idea at all to borrow and repay small loans periodically to establish your reputation and credit rating with several (not just one) banks. When they know you, from past successful business dealings, you may get an open line of credit for your use as needed. It is a very good safety net to have ready and waiting for emergency situations beyond your control, and the big business cycle is one of them. Prepare for the storm before it strikes, so you can live through one, and be

STEERING CLEAR OF FINANCIAL PITFALLS

ready to rebound into the marketplace lean, hungry, but still alive and with fewer competitors to contend with as well.

In summary then, what are some financial mistakes you can make that can and will cause the small business some problems?

1. Undercapitalization.
2. Poor or no cost control.
3. Confusing growth with profit. You grow too fast and run short of cash to support and maintain your expansion.
4. Slow collection of your accounts receivables or bad debts.
5. You spend money just because it is available instead of saving as much as you can as rapidly as you can.
6. You concentrate your interests and efforts entirely within your own small world and forget about or ignore the big economic picture. The general business cycle can affect you. You can't control it, but you can blunt its effect upon you if you plan ahead.
7. You make business plans, but no financial plan to fund them.
8. You tie up your funds in fixed assets or to pay for your loan debts. These are fixed obligations that are difficult or may even be impossible to change later, when you need the funds for other purposes.

6

BEWARE OF THESE SEVEN OPERATIONAL WRONGS

NOW WE GET to the third and fourth management functions: direction and control. These everyday operations set the real tone of your operations and in the end result in your success and growth or loss of contracts, unhappy clients, and the slow death of your company. Mistakes made here are not as dramatic or as fixed and unchangeable as other more serious and permanent errors. However, any mistake can hurt you, and, if left unattended, can become more serious. Suddenly, a major contract is cancelled or a number of your key employees resign and leave you in deep trouble. These mistakes are generally small and may slip by, due to your concern about other, more important matters at the moment.

INFORMAL STARTUP

The small outfit starts out very informally with the owner and a few personnel, who are all on a friendly first-name basis. It is almost like a family. Everyone does what has to be done and the camaraderie is wonderful to behold, but it won't last. It can't and should not as you start to grow. Some of your original staff may resent and resist your attempts to formalize your business and make it more like other going concerns. They liked the informality of the very small business and their direct access to you. Their efficiency may drop off as you grow.

Some typical operational mistakes that small business entrepreneurs make are:

SEVEN OPERATIONAL WRONGS 87

1. Staying informal too long.
2. Retaining all control.
3. Poor direction and control.
4. Business decisions made for nonbusiness reasons.
5. The folly of nepotism.
6. Operational problems are not quickly corrected.
7. Repeating past mistakes.

FORMALIZE AS QUICKLY AS YOU CAN

The easy informality of the small business office should end as your outfit grows. A procedure for proper direction and control of the operation on a day-to-day basis should replace the "see the boss" system as soon as possible. Quick word of mouth direction on the spot is fine, however it leads to mistakes, misunderstandings, confusion, arguments, and inefficiency. I am not a bureaucrat, in fact I don't particularly like bureaucratic activity at all, and I am not an advocate of paperwork and formal procedures as ends in themselves. However, procedures that serve a useful purpose and increase understanding and efficiency are good.

Generally, formalization is forced upon small businesses by outside pressures. A big job comes in and you have no written schedules, budgets, defined responsibilities, or progress reporting procedures. This leads to confusion and some semiformal procedures start to emerge by necessity. It is better to plan it. Do it from the top down, not from the bottom up. Owners may be able to operate with ten or fewer people and personally monitor and control everything, but they will be very busy people. Also, most of their attention will be drawn inward and downward to solve many minor internal problems; i.e., ordering supplies, helping people do their jobs, answering questions, and supervising the shop. Let your supervisors do these things so you can have time to look and concentrate outward towards new business, growth, and new clients. If the owner concentrates on internal daily operations to complete the current job, when this job is done, there is no new job for everyone to work on, and it is all over.

I know one owner who ran his outfit like the captain of a team, not the coach. He was very sports oriented. Each day he and his employees would get coffee and spend 45 minutes discussing the sports scene. They all loved it. He had a company softball team and he was the leader/manager of the team. They won the championship, were awarded a big trophy, defeated their client's team in league playoffs (never beat your client at anything), and said they were Number 1. I asked this fellow, "Number 1 what?" They were Number 1 in softball, but the client did not renew the work contract. The employees really liked this guy. He was very popular with them, but they did not have any new work to do. He led them right off a cliff. They were all too interested in sports, taking their lead from their boss, who acted as if sports were more important at work than work. I like sports too, but my wife suffers because of it. It has no place in my business world. I do it at home.

I strongly suggest you keep your hobbies, sports, personal matters, and other nonbusiness topics away from your office or factory. Work with one group and relax and play with another. Don't mix them up. Another owner was a bridge player, so he organized card games during lunch hour and he and his employees' lunch hours would extend up to two hours to complete an interesting card game. He told me that he liked to relax in the middle of the day. He did and so did all of his employees. I suggested that he start his bridge games at 5:00 P.M. each day and see how many would stay and play cards with him.

Situations like these are not going to happen in a big outfit, but they are quite common in the small outfit. The owner/boss has some special or even peculiar interest and since he or she runs the store now, all of the employees join in and little work gets done. They follow the leader.

Also, the top person in any outfit tends to be viewed as a parent figure regardless of age. Informal, personal discussions arise in which the employees seek out and talk with the boss about subjects that really have no place in the business world.

It is an easy trap to fall into and difficult to escape from later. I know, I fell into it and found I was spending up to several hours a day with employees on their personal nonjob related problems. They were lining up to see me as in a doctor's office. I backed off when a woman tried to seek my advice about her child who was on drugs. I did not know what to tell her. Another asked me if he should divorce his errant wife or not. I told him I had enough difficulty trying to keep my own life in order, and I was not qualified to advise anyone on such serious personal subjects like that. He also asked me if our company fringe-benefit package paid for legal expenses for divorces.

When I abruptly stopped this informal practice, it created resentment amongst the employees. I had gotten in over my head and it was difficult to get back into shallow water. I strongly suggest that you don't start such things, because you are not qualified to be a father confessor or psychiatrist. You are practicing without a license. Next, it does not help your business at all, does it? You need your energy to make your company succeed, not be a guidance counselor. Get big fast and hire these qualified people to work in your personnel or medical department and they can do it right.

Don't make the mistake of being too informal or too intimate with the employees. Familiarity does breed contempt and that is not good for you personally or for your business venture. When big clients visit your office to discuss business, they will judge you in part by what they see and hear. If they observe a neat, quiet, efficient office, similar to their own, that is good for you. Impressions do matter, and if they come in and hear radios on, and a 19-year old receptionist calls you and says "Hey, Joe, some guy is here to see you," then your visitor may be disturbed by that sort of "informality." It may just cost you a new job.

In our early years, a client of ours, who fortunately was also a former associate, called me on the telephone about a new contract. He said, "Bill, some guy just answered your telephone and said, "It's your dime—shoot." The receptionist had left her desk and one of our Ph.D. senior analysts had answered the telephone. What an impression he gave to our client. I had to write an office memo to advise people if they answered the office telephone to say, "Good morning (or afternoon), ACSI, may I help you?"

Your business clients have every right to judge you by their standards, not yours. Office informality is generally judged by the outside world as inefficiency or indifference, no matter how good your product or service is. Everything that exists contains form and substance. Substance is by far the most important, but form, format, or procedures are many times given priority over substance. The wrapping on the package is, many times, just as or even more important than the contents. It should not be that way, but it is. Your product or service is your substance, but the way you direct and control your operations is your style or form; this shows first, like the wrapping on the gift. Clients may negatively judge your informal format, so that they do not even bother to open the package to see that the substance inside is of great value.

Your informal, sleeves-up attitude may get the job done, but what impression does it give to the outside business world? People will judge you on perceptions whether you like it or not. You can always get more and more informal as you like, but it is difficult to go the other way as you grow. It is best to start out the way you want it to be when you grow. You will find that, as you grow, it tends to get more formal anyway. It has to. That is the way it is. The choice is yours. You do it now easily or you do it later, the hard way. I have done it both ways, and, in my opinion, it is better to be more than less formal in your daily office procedures. It creates a much better business atmosphere for all concerned.

DELEGATE! YOU CAN'T DO IT ALL

Owners staying in the saddle, like John Wayne, for too long can be a big mistake and hurt or inhibit their companies' growth and expansion. This is a common mistake that many of us make early on. You want everything to be perfect (which it never is, of course), and you end up working 80 hours a week and complaining that no one will help you. The reason is you won't let anyone help you.

You started the new venture (I hope) to prosper and succeed and then live to enjoy the fruits of your labor. If they carry you out feet first due to overwork and too much worry, I don't see what good it all did for you, do you? Formalize your setup, direct and control it from above, and have others do the work. You manage it. You must allow others to do the job their way. You may tell them what you want and when, but leave the "how" to them. Let them plan it and submit the plan to you for approval. If it looks OK, let the supervisor or manager take it from there. Doing it yourself, especially if you do and redo the things you know, doesn't help you learn anything new. Let someone else do it who is taking a job off your shoulders, and who is also learning and growing at the same time because it is new for them. Here is the hard part. They will make mistakes. Just make sure they are not catastrophic or deadly ones. This is the essence of good judgment and good management. When do you let them work their own way out and when do you directly intervene, take over, and put it right. Be careful if and when you take over. You can damage fragile egos and they do not recover easily. Only you know when and how to do this. If you do it well, you succeed, if you don't, you fail.

Let's assume that you are wonderful and you do everything right the first time. You are a one-man band. You will start fast, succeed quickly, but sooner or later you cannot continue growing because you can't do it all. At this stage new work is coming in due to your masterful performance on current and completed contracts. Now you have no middle level managers or supervisors ready to help you manage, because you never had any in training on current or former jobs. Now, by necessity, you must delegate and you don't want to, and your managers know this, so they will be reluctant to make any decisions without your prior approval. You won't grow that way, will you?

I know an entrepreneur who built up his small outfit from zero to $5 million in annual sales and his company had a fine reputation. He was approached by a very big outfit to buy him out at a price of $7.5 million. He was very excited and happy, but, as the negotiations progressed, and the buyer's people looked into his operation in detail, they found no real organization or control. It was, as they said, a one-man operation. They withdrew their offer, and he is still plugging away, working seven days a week doing three or four different jobs. He is still in the saddle, but he is 55 years old and getting tired. He earns a very nice six-figure income, but he can't go away with his family for vacations. He can only grab a few days at a time. What is he a candidate for? He knows, but he won't change.

You should free yourself up from everyday work as soon as you possibly can. Direct your attentions to outside areas (i.e., new work, hiring new personnel) and your future plans. If you cannot find time to think six months or a year ahead and you are mired down in daily problems, look carefully at your company. Are you addressing immediate, serious problems that really require your constant daily attention, or are you just refusing to let go and be what you are supposed to be, the leader and general manager of your company?

You will have to let go sooner or later. Will you do it willingly by your plan or have it happen by outside pressures or by pressure from below? As said before, plan from the top down, not from the bottom up. Hanging on too long and trying to do it all is counterproductive, or worse, it can kill you and your corporation.

CHANGE CAN CAUSE CONFUSION

Poor direction and control is another common small business mistake that can cause serious problems. This stems from the general informality of any new venture and the sudden and drastic changes that accrue to any operation that can grow or contract suddenly due to changing business conditions. Like the human baby, the small company can double in size during each year or two at the start. Rapid change tends to lead to changing jobs, new responsibilities, and employees handling

SEVEN OPERATIONAL WRONGS 93

two or more entirely different jobs, so direction and control becomes very difficult. An owner may be chief engineer and treasurer, have a daily responsibility to get production out and a corporate responsibility to handle the company's finances. He or she becomes confused, has no direction from above, and mistakes occur. What are his or her priorities?

One treasurer/engineer let $100,000 sit in the corporate checking account drawing no interest for two months because he was busy doing his day-to-day job. Checks coming in were just deposited in the checking account and earned no interest. When he was told to buy 30-day Certificates of Deposits, he did, and he started to earn interest on these funds. It was a question of loose direction and no control. Such things, unfortunately, are all too common in the new small business. For example, $100,000 at 12 percent earns $1,000 per month. Why lose it because of loose controls and no direction? It is your outfit and when you make a mistake, you pay the price.

If possible, every five to eight people should have a supervisor. A manager should be assigned for every five supervisors, and a senior manager for every five middle managers. That is a good span of control. The military uses it. In addition to verbal direction, a written schedule for all jobs should be prepared and monitored daily by the supervisors, and weekly by the managers. Written progress reports prepared every Friday should be prepared by all personnel up to the top person in the company. Direction comes down through channels and progress reports go up. This is the way you get feedback so you can adjust and control your operations. If done properly, each manager or supervisor reads five to eight one-page progress reports and prepares his own to report against the schedule and budget.

A word about progress reports is in order. At first, we let each person write his or her own progress report. We got back some one-line reports which said nothing and some four or five page stories that must have taken all day Friday to compose. Generally, the longer the progress report, the less progress was made. People feel compelled to justify themselves when they do not get the work done. Any teacher or professor can tell you that the longer the answer, the less the person knows about the question. They write at length looking for partial credit about what they do know, even if it is not what you want to hear or see.

Make out your own progress report form and insist each line is filled in and each question is answered. Leave a space for problem areas and also look for things the report should say, but does not. Few of us like to admit we need help or that we did something wrong. That is the managers' job to determine when they read the weekly progress reports.

These progress reports also serve another very useful function. When your managers recommend someone for a raise or promotion, take out their last six month's progress reports and read them, one after the other. You may get an entirely different view of this person's value and contributions, than your manager holds. You can also judge the value of your managers and determine if they know who merits the raises and promotions, based on performance and not on whom they like and whom they don't like. Part of any manager's job is to spot and reward outstanding performers and, without your progress reports, you have to act on what they say about someone. All managers are not fair and impartial. Our progress reporting system uncovered two poor managers whom we were able to identify and remove before they did any serious damage. The employees' progress reports indicated a slippage in schedule in one case, and the manager's reports never mentioned it. In the other case, the employees' reports indicated confusion, misdirection, and misunderstanding about the job and the manager's reports never mentioned any problems at all. Higher management would never have been made aware of these problems without the feedback of written, weekly progress reports in time to head off what would have been serious problems in a few months' time.

FORMAL PROCEDURES

How you direct and control your own outfit is up to you, but formal, written procedures do help, whatever system you select to follow. Once again, you will end up doing it sooner or later, either by your own plan or after some big mistake or customer complaint comes to you. Why not start out doing it from day one? That is one thing we did right even though I met with some resistance when we had only seven employees, and we knew what each was doing everyday, anyway. I carried over the procedures we used when I worked for the big outfits and used a similar system. I did not use a prepared format until I got tired of reading long science fiction stories each week in which some of our employees were writing about their own feelings and illnesses on the progress reports. A quick change to a one page format fixed that up.

Direction and control mistakes can be corrected if your basic plan and organization are sound, because poor direction or poor or no control shows up pretty quickly when little things go wrong each day. Catch them early so they won't add up and bury you. The best way to keep on top of it is by close monitoring and the best method of monitoring is via the written progress report. It is the oil that lubricates the system. It is your internal communication system by which you "tweak," twist, and fine-tune your small business.

POWER CORRUPTS—BE CAREFUL!

Small business owners are free to run their companies any way they like. With no authority or manager over them and no need to justify any business actions, some may make decisions based on personal whim or for nonvalid or nonexistent business reasons. This is another rather common mistake some small business people make. Do this at your peril. Any decisions or actions either at home or at work based on your feelings or emotions generally don't work out too well, do they? Promoting an unqualified, old, faithful retainer, who has loyally supported you since day one, does the employee no good and can seriously damage your growing business as well. Take care of him or her in some other way. Don't put your employees in over their heads because you feel you "owe it to them."

As you grow, a different type of person may be needed for the new, big contract and it is better to hire in new, fully qualified personnel than to try to promote from within, when your small staff does not contain anyone qualified for the management position. I made the mistake of giving management and supervisory positions to about ten or twelve technical men and women, and all but two failed and I had to demote, transfer, or reassign them back to their former level. This was a bad scene. Some resigned while some became embarrassed and stayed on knowing no more promotion possibilities existed for them into management. In most cases, I knew "deep down" they could not manage, but they wanted the chance. My heart ruled my head and I acted on my emotions instead of in a business-like manner.

Favoritism exists anywhere, but in the long run it is not effective. If you hire friends (we will get to relatives in the next section) and promote them on that basis, I can assure you one or two things will happen. You will lose them as friends, or they will do some damage to your small venture. When anyone can count on the boss to forgive and forget, no matter what is accomplished, stand by for trouble. The company you lose may be your own.

Keep an eye out for office romances. You may think that what consenting adults do after working hours is none of your business, but if you think a torrid romance can heat up after 5:00 P.M. and cool off by 8:00 A.M. on the next day, and not in any way affect on-the-job performance, then you also believe in the tooth fairy. If the participants are married, but not to each other, then you may hear loud and clear from the offended spouse. Do you need this at any time? Well, ignore it and see what happens, and you may be in it right up to your ears. Some years ago, an affair was going on right in front of me and I did not see it. There are none so blind as those who will not see. My secretary alerted me and told me to watch Mr. X and Mrs. Y. I did and all the signs were there. The sly glances, the secret smiles, coincidental "sick leave," and long absences during the lunch hour were all occurring. They were having an affair and I was paying them while they did it. What a deal for them. It took me several weeks to get up the courage to address the problem. That was some years ago. Today I could and would act immediately and let them be embarrassed, not me.

In any case, I spoke to them separately and told each that we all knew what was going on and it had better stop once and for all. Both quietly resigned.

Such romances can turn sour and not only does on-the-job performance suffer, sexual harassment may occur as a result. Federal and state laws are now very specific on the subject. The company can clearly be held responsible, if it does not make a clear public policy that sexual harassment won't be tolerated and severe discipline will follow, up to and including dismissal. We published such a policy, and sure enough a romance turned sour. The complaint came in to me via a client, who observed two of our personnel who were working some distance away from my office. We quickly invoked our previously published policy on the subject with appropriate discipline, and it ended then and there.

All this has absolutely nothing to do with making your company grow, and it can all be very distracting to you. The courts are very active today; a lawsuit from a former friend or lover who now claims that his or her demotion or dismissal was not for valid business reasons can cost you plenty. Do you want some judge ordering you to reinstate Mary or Joe for nine months' back pay and restored to his or her former position when you don't want them to work for you? It has happened. Don't let it happen to you. Do your hiring, promotions, transfers, and especially your dismissals for strictly business reasons, and you won't have any trouble. Play favorites and use your emotions, in lieu of your best business judgment of what is best for your company, and you may go too far off the track. You will make mistakes, we all do. Fortunately there are no laws to punish you for making a mistake, for, if there were, there would not be enough jails to hold us all.

NEPOTISM! DON'T DO IT

Nepotism comes from French and Italian words that mean nephew. In English, it means favoring relatives, especially in getting them jobs. This is perhaps the most serious operational mistake a small business entrepreneur can make. The odds against any small business are great anyway, however when you throw nepotism into the pot, you really tilt the odds against survival.

"Don't do business with relatives or friends" is a good general rule to follow. You may well be able to point to an individual case in which Smith & Sons make it big, but, in far more cases than not, when Smith brought in his sons, the company suffered. One of our early clients was Jones Electronics (not the real name). We were doing payrolls for small businesses then. Jones Electronics had about 30 employees. One day the fellow who ran the computer for us told me that 17 of the people who worked for Jones Electronics were named Jones. What a family affair! The company lasted for about nine months, and owed us for three months' services when they closed the doors. This was nepotism gone mad.

I have never met anyone who says he believes in nepotism, however the same person will hire family members. I read an executive survey in which 90 percent of the executives said nepotism was bad, yet 76 percent of the same executives said they have and would employ relatives in their organization. Please believe me, it is not a good thing to do. When any of the bosses' family shows up for work, it puts a strain on the whole outfit, whether or not they are good at their jobs or work hard.

Correcting a mistake made here is more difficult than normal, because it extends beyond the office door and into your home. Please remember, you may think that your kids and relatives are the greatest, but you are wrong. Mine are! Joe thinks his are! Mix relatives and business and you have just made a time bomb that is ticking away, waiting to explode at the worst possible time. Since you never know in advance how such things will work out, be smart and play the percentages. David did defeat Goliath once, in their first encounter, but if there ever is a rematch, bet on Goliath. Small businesses need all the help they can get, so why make it more difficult for yourself when you have got enough to do elsewhere? I don't have to give any examples to describe this situation. You already know of some, don't you? If you think yours is a special case, as we all tend to think, think again. Are you making the decision for good business reasons, or is it for emotional or nonbusiness reasons?

BE QUICK! IT'S YOUR BIGGEST ASSET

Perhaps the greatest advantage the small business has over big corporations is speed. You are quick and you can react immediately to an ever changing situation, to correct a mistake or to grasp a fleeting opportunity. Giving up this great advantage, for whatever reason, is dangerous. Why should you slow down and retard your progress and give away your greatest advantage? No one does it deliberately, of course, but some do actually become slow and lethargic, like the big outfits. Being impatient and nervous by nature, I have never had any trouble about being too slow to decide or act. Amongst my other human faults, those who choose to "help" me with constructive criticism tell me that many times I move and decide too quickly. I apologize and accept this criticism, but I still do it because, on average, I know I have gained far more than I have lost by moving quickly. When most of us have any fear, doubt, or uncertainty, we tend to pause, ponder, and become inactive. Fear of making a mistake, fear of change, or fear of others criticizing you makes you pause and reflect far too long.

Goofing off is another operational mistake that can be fatal to the small business. Before you dismiss this out of hand and say that no one who runs his or her own small business would deliberately goof off, permit me to respectfully disagree. It all goes back to your basic reason for starting your own small venture. If you are in it to make the maximum amount of money in the shortest period of time so you can retire to the good life at 45 or 50, you won't goof off. It is not in your plan. However, many do not run their own small business for that reason. Some want the freedom to be their own boss, work when and where they choose, and select and reject work on a subjective basis of what is interesting to them. These entrepreneurs tend to "goof off" and slow down and actually refuse new business. It is your outfit to do with as you please, however if you work in or for a small outfit, you won't go too far working for an owner/boss who wants to slow down and take it easy. The competition is not slowing down while your company stalls, and sales will level off and eventually drop.

NO SELF-DISCIPLINE

I have seen the part owner of a nice growing company start to come in late one hour every morning, take long lunch hours, and go home early. In addition, he would be absent three Mondays out of four. His average time per week spent in the office was under 25 hours. When his other owner/partners asked him about this, he said he was nearing 50 years of age and it was time to slow down, relax, and enjoy other things. He was counting on the other owners to take up the slack and carry on while he rested, relaxed, and enjoyed himself. This sort of thing can destroy otherwise successful companies. One or several of the owners turn their interest elsewhere. Another Ph.D. I know got a nice software consulting company going. He was up to 18 employees, and he told me he would not go over 20. It would take up too much of his time if he grew too large. He bought a boat and spent much time during the so-called work week cruising around in his boat. He worked when and how he pleased. He had it made, but only temporarily. The last recession put him out of business, after ten years of the "good life." He slowed down too soon, started to coast, turned away new work, became nonresponsive and even unavailable to his clients. So, they just shifted to another outfit that was quick, responsive, and ready to please and satisfy the client.

If you let your small outfit become sluggish and resistant to change because you like things the way they are right now, please remember that change is an inherent part of business. It is almost impossible to grow to a predetermined size and remain there as my Ph.D. associate tried to do. It cost him dearly. You either go up or down in sales, you do not remain constant.

ADMIT YOUR MISTAKES AND LEARN SOMETHING

We all make mistakes, but do you learn from them? Some mistakes are fatal per se and you do not get a second chance, and other mistakes can be corrected. Operational mistakes are mostly correctable, as said earlier, however if you insist on repeating the same mistakes over and over again, even minor mistakes, repeated often enough, can have the same cumulative fatal impact as one big catastrophic mistake.

"Typical" small business entrepreneurs tend to be hard headed, because they went ahead and did what few others dared to do. They actually went out and started their own new venture, so their initial success or even surviving in the face of high odds proves to them that they were right to do what they did. Fine, but this sort of thought process leads to rigidity. Some problem develops, they attack it and make a mistake. Instead of learning from the mistake, they back off and, like an angry bull, they charge ahead and make the same mistake all over again. It worked before, so they will keep plugging away until the resistance is overcome. It is very difficult to convince entrepreneurs who have prospered and grown for several years that they have made a number of mistakes and some changes should be made to correct them so the company can grow at an accelerated pace. The foregoing six types of operational mistakes mean nothing to someone who either:

1. Refuses to admit that the problem exists.
2. Admits it exists, but doesn't want to do anything about it.
3. Thinks time alone will automatically solve it.
4. Cannot distinguish between a minor mistake and a catastrophic mistake.

THE REPEATER

Whatever the reason, the result is you have a "repeater" who never learns and does it over again until the bankruptcy court puts an end to it once and for all. Even in the extreme case of bankruptcy, I have seen entrepreneurs who want to go right out and try to do it again in exactly the same way. Anyone admires persistence (to be presented in Chapter 11), however the difference between persistence and being just plain bullheaded is judgment, and you will not get good judgment by starting a business. You either did or did not get it early in life. Later in life, you just manifest and display your good judgment or lack of same. If your basic idea and plan are good, stick to them, but be pragmatic about how you achieve your end or goal.

I am not saying that the end justifies the means in a moral sense. If you do something morally or legally wrong or hurt and injure someone, that is wrong. You cannot justify your actions because the goal you were after was noble, honorable, and good. If your accountant stole $200,000 from you and donated it all to charity for the needy, is that OK with you? I doubt it. I am advocating the pragmatic approach for any organization, the direction and control system that helps you implement your plan and reach your goal. If it works, use it. If not, be ready to quickly discard it, try something else, and go on from there. In order to be pragmatic and receptive to new things and change, you have to be able to quickly admit that there is a better way than what you have done or are doing. In other words, you must easily accept the fact that you are not wonderful, and you make mistakes too. Never be completely satisfied. People who are satisfied don't want to change anything. What for, if it is great right now? Let's just keep everything as is, for as long as possible. Dangerous thoughts for the small venture.

STAY TUNED IN

There are as many ways to make mistakes as there are people. Many times, operational mistakes do give you early warning, if you are tuned in and they register on your "Richter Scale." Many can be anticipated if you look ahead a bit and think about it. If you must make mistakes, make them in the areas of direction and control, rather than fatal mistakes that cannot be repaired.

In summary then, what are some of the operational mistakes you can make to cause the small outfit some problems?

1. Get too close to your personnel on a personal basis.
2. Have a too informal operation.

3. Do it all yourself and refuse to delegate.
4. Make business decisions for nonbusiness reasons.
5. Hire relatives and close personal friends.
6. Become slow and lethargic and not respond to your clients as quickly as you can.
7. Divert your interests elsewhere.
8. Keep making the same mistakes over and over again.

7

PREVENTIVE REMEDIES FOR GROWTH PAINS

THE MAIN PROBLEM with most small businesses is no growth or a decline or cessation of sales altogether. Sales are the lifeblood of any small or big business operation. No matter how wonderful you are personally, how good you are to your employees, or how excellent your product or service is, unless you can sell it to someone and on a regular, sustained basis, your company will die. That is plain enough to understand, isn't it? Yet many small business entrepreneurs seem to forget this plain fact of business life. Many pay little or at best grudging attention to sales and growth. They like the technical work or some other aspect of their jobs, and, since they now have no boss to order them around, they do exactly what they please. Many truly and honestly believe at first that their superior product or service will "speak for itself," and when the world finds out about it, the world will beat a path to their door. That may be true if you make mousetraps, but it is not true for anything else. So, if you don't produce mousetraps, you have to go out and get customers; they will not line up at your door. A major and often deadly mistake a small business entrepreneur can make is not concentrating constantly on sales and new business and opportunities for growth.

SELL VALUE, NOT EFFORT

One of our senior analysts told me that when our client sees the excellent software that his department prepared for use within the deliverable hardware, the client would be so impressed that we would get more work from this "impressed" client. I told our manager the client does not give a damn about a beautiful software package. The client wants only to push some buttons and get the job done, and if it works, fine; if not, there are complaints. You won't sell software services or any other kind of services or product by trying to show the client how wonderful your work is. You sell results, not effort; thinking only in terms of your effort won't help you grow.

Another growth mistake a small business person can make is to tell your client how badly you need the work, because you will have to lay people off, if the customer or client does not "give you a break" and give you the job. If you try this on any client or new customer, I can guarantee about a 99 and 44/100 percent failure to get the job right then and there. Would you sign a sizable contract with anyone who admitted to you that he or she desperately needed your job to stave off financial disaster? In addition, the entrepreneur asks for your special consideration and understanding because he or she is just starting out or has been in business only one or two years. Would you give it to this firm and hope for the best, to help this new venture get its feet on the ground? Most of us want to deal with an ongoing business with a good, solid reputation based on past performance. The chances are that this company will repeat with another good job to further enhance its reputation and add another satisfied client to its list.

Some of our major clients' personnel have told me some incredible stories in which some people have actually cried and begged for work to stay in business. I asked these senior client representatives did they ever respond to such requests? They all said, "Yes"; they responded by politely getting the supplicant out of their offices as soon as possible. They would never deal with an "unstable" contractor who was on the verge of going under. So, don't cry for help from your potential clients; not only will it not help you grow, they will spread the word to other potential clients who then won't even see you when you try to make an appointment.

Look at it from the clients' point of view, not yours. They are going to pay you money to do something for them, right? Why should they deal with you at all? You must convince them it is to their advantage to do business with you. It certainly does not hurt if they know you and also like you. This will not guarantee that you will get the job; it only means they will listen to you and knowing you and your reputation, they will believe you. But, you had better deliver later, per the terms and conditions of your contract with them, or else you won't get any follow-up work. Friendship only goes so far. Now if they know you, but they don't particularly like you, this will just about guarantee that you won't get even one job. I have seen more than one client look for ways to not do business with a small business entrepreneur because the client's personnel don't like him or her. Unfortunately the "reasons" for personal dislike are subjective and may have nothing to do with your company's performance or capability.

DON'T LET IT SHOW TOO SOON

The lesson to be learned here is don't let your prosperity show too soon to your clients and the world. It can adversely affect your growth opportunities. People are people, and whether we like it or not, some get jealous and will act on their feelings. The price of your service or product should be what matters, not what you do with the money you receive, but this is not always true. When my employees defeated the client's staff in a league softball game, the client was upset. If you show that your standard of living is higher than your client's personnel, who actually select who gets the contract, this can affect your future sales and growth from that client. In most cases, if it happens to you, your clients will not openly and directly tell you why. They know jealousy is not a good business reason to deny you the contract, so they will quietly find other "reasons" to eliminate your company from additional contracts.

This situation is not at all rare. The previously mentioned Ph.D. who sailed his big boat around Marblehead Harbor created resentment among his clients, who could not afford to buy and operate such a luxury. I know this because our company was dealing with one of his clients at the time and we heard complaints about it. Should anyone buying a new car or a new boat have any affect on your growth opportunities? Absolutely not, but it does.

I always take part of my vacation in February when the kids are on February vacation. I am getting old and I don't like snow. We all go to Bermuda for a week to escape the cold weather. It is no more expensive than taking a week's vacation anywhere, but I well remember one time when I returned to work in late February and went to visit one of our clients with a nice tan. He looked at me and asked where did I get the tan in mid-February? Foolishly, I told him and he erupted right in front of me and said, "You are getting rich on my money and I cannot afford such a vacation." I still go on vacation, but on return I do not go to see my clients until my tan fades away. It takes only a week or so.

REFUSING NEW JOBS

Turning away new jobs that are offered to you will, in most cases, end all future possibilities for new work from that client forever. When, as will sometimes happen, an unsolicited new business opportunity arises, think twice before you refuse it. It is unexpected and it is not in your current business plan; but here is your opportunity to show a new client, or an old client who calls you for additional work, your business savvy. These clients know you had not planned on their call, so if they see you react, adjust, and respond to their requests with such short notice, they will be prone to call you again. If you refuse, or try to "put them on hold," or worse, you just ignore them, forget it! You will never hear from them again. If you call for a taxi and Company A never has any cabs available, but Company B usually responds immediately, you will very soon stop calling Company A, won't you?

We have had a client since 1970 and it is our oldest and best continuing account. It all started with a telephone call from a former associate, who asked if we could provide his group with two senior software engineers. After much argument with one of my managers, who did not want to disrupt his staff and have to hire and train two replacements, I sent two of our best people. It developed into our biggest, most lucrative and enduring contract. If it ended today (which I hope and pray it won't), it was still worth it for many years of consistent and expanding growth and sales.

Another mistake you can make that adversely affects growth is in your pricing, and I do not mean too high a price, I mean too low. In the attempts to enter the market and capture a badly needed contract, some will deliberately price their product or service at a price so low that, in their minds, will result in their winning the badly needed job. There are two unfortunate things that can happen to you if you try this. The first one is very quick and painful. The client decides your price is so low that you don't know what you are doing and you don't get the job. The second one is you do get the job, but you are unable to do it for the price you quoted. Now you have two options, to do it at a loss or to go back and try to convince the client to increase the price during the period of performance. You have to do some fast talking and most clients do not like this. Either one of these options results from underpricing to get your foot in the door. It is a dangerous ploy.

IT'S DIFFICULT TO RAISE THE PRICE

In addition, let's assume that you do the first job well and for a minimum price. Now the client wants some additional work from you. If you think you can now get a reasonable price because you have proven yourself, think again my friend. Your client sees you increase your costs by 25 percent or so and the fee rate is now 12 percent instead of 6 percent as for the first job. You tell the client you are just trying to get the fair "going rate." That is how you see it. The client sees it differently. The client thinks that, just because you did a good job for him or her, you are going to capitalize upon this and "stick it" to him or her with a big price increase. If you think only the total billing price counts, think again. Many clients will demand to see your cost, overhead, and fee structure. If you do any business with the government, this information is mandatory; you won't get the contract unless you provide it. The initial low price is called the "buy in." All clients, especially the government, are on the alert for any contractor "buying in" at an obviously low price, and planning to get it back as the work progresses via various nefarious schemes. Even if you succeed once, this sort of thing gives your company a bad reputation. In future procurements, the clients will never believe or accept your price. This greatly inhibits your opportunity for growth. Still many try it to get started and get into all sorts of financial and legal difficulties later on. They take their shot and hope for the best.

SET YOUR PRICE

Our first contract was 90 days from completion when we submitted a competitive bid for a bigger job to the same client (the federal government). If we did not win it, we would have gone of out of business. My business associate was so afraid of not getting the new job that he wanted to price it so low that we would have been operating at a loss. My position was, if we cannot compete in a competitive market and make a fair profit, the sooner we find out the better. After much arguing, I ignored him and submitted our planned costs, overhead, and a 10 percent fee. Fortunately, we won the award and survived, but if I had succumbed to my manager's fears and got the same job at far too low a price, just what would we have gained? If you have to play tricks or operate below your actual costs, you are going to fail sooner or later, aren't you?

Now let's jump to the other extreme; you try to grow too fast. As said earlier, growth per se is not always good, nor does it always produce a profit. Growing too fast is a problem that 99 out of 100 new business entrepreneurs would gladly take on when they are struggling to maintain their low sales base and worrying about staying alive for the next six months. You can choke when you bite off too big a piece of the pie and try to swallow it too quickly, all in one big piece. Companies have choked to death in the same way. It is extremely difficult for a new company to deliberately turn down a big opportunity that falls their way. Here is where your discipline and good judgment are called upon. It is time to review and perhaps redo your basic business plan, reorganize, hire new staff, and direct and control an entirely new job; you have only 30 days to start. It is the opportunity of a lifetime. It can double or quadruple your sales in a year or so. Wonderful! Can you do it? If you try and fail, it is all over.

Disordered and too rapid growth in the human body produces serious medical problems and even death. Disordered and too rapid growth in the corporate body can be just as fatal. Such a big chance is almost irresistible to a small business owner. He or she probably won't ever get such a chance again, especially from the company that wants the work done. Our work seemed to come in bite-size pieces, and the work got bigger in stages that were digestible. I guess that was more by chance than by plan, but, even so, our company officers had their most violent arguments over how to expand to staff new work and grow. I well remember how difficult it was, because these arguments got very personal; to this day, the scars remain, and all over the opportunity to increase sales, profit, and growth. I shudder to think what would have happened to us if, early on, we were presented with an opportunity to suddenly grow from 25 to 50 employees due to the winning of one new contract. It is my considered opinion that if we had been offered such an opportunity, I would have received violent opposition from other company officers who would have wanted to accept the new job, and we would have failed.

GROWING WITHOUT PROFIT

The stresses and strains on the corporate body to respond and adjust to sudden and large expansion are great. You need more money fast. You have to replan and readjust your priorities. You have to reorganize and hire a number of new people in a hurry. You have to "digest" the new people, train them, fit them into an entirely new working structure. Old procedures must go. Some do not want to change, so you get pulled in many directions, all calling for your immediate attention. Some have been able to successfully pull off a very sudden and large corporate growth, but I know I could not do it successfully.

Even in very large companies, rapid expansion is very difficult. A close friend who is a general manager of a very large corporate division with $350 million in annual sales, won a very large new government contract for several hundred million dollars over a three-year period. He put in 80-hour, seven-day weeks for over a year, trying to hire staff, get it going, satisfy his new client, find new qualified middle-management personnel, and somehow add 250 people to his staff. At this writing, he still does not have it in shape. He is a very talented and gifted manager; there are not many around who are as good as he is, or as devoted and motivated. This guy is top drawer all the way, and he is going flat out to increase his division by approximately 33 percent. I am not as good a manager as he is, and I don't think many small business people are either, so I can postulate that most of us would be even more hard pressed to successfully manage a 50 percent or 100 percent increase in size of our small companies in a year or two.

More small businesses fail due to lack of business than from having too much. However, in either case, when a company dies, the reason is of no real value to the company, only to those corporate coroners who examine the remains and write brilliant articles and books explaining it all in the King's English for the benefit of those who will follow. If your reason for being in business is to make a profit, don't pursue growth per se. A 100 percent increase in sales does not automatically mean a 100 percent increase in profit. On the contrary, a sudden expansion could drain all available cash from your company and force you into the money market at very high interest rates; or you may go public, sell off 40 percent of your company at very low prices, and if, as you expand and you watch your over-the-counter stock go up in price, you think the shares that you hold are of equal value, well, we will discuss this in Chapter 9. You may now be a millionaire on paper, but wait until you try to cash in your shares. You may be in for a very unpleasant surprise.

DIMINISHING RETURNS

As you add to your staff to handle your expanding work, there is another problem to watch out for, and that is your newly recruited people may not be as responsive, as productive, or as "tuned in" as your "old hands." Slowly but surely, things do not get done as quickly or as well as before. Loose ends appear, and your quiet orders and directives that formerly resulted in immediate and efficient action don't get done as quickly or are ignored. There are many reasons for this phenomenon. Some are:

- The law of diminishing returns is starting to affect you and your operation.
- The new employees don't know you from the early days and they have no personal rapport with you.
- Many new employees will carry over their work habits from their former place of employment.

You can't do anything about the law of diminishing returns. It appears to be as natural as gravity, so you just have to watch out for its arrival and plan your work with the law in mind. For example, if you estimate that a job will take four people six months to do, that is a 24-man/months job. If you plan to get the job done in three months and you assign eight people to do it, you are in for an overrun. Time has a price. If the optimum way to do this job is in six months with four people, and you want it done in three months, regardless of the cost, then it may take ten or eleven people to buy you the needed three month's time. If you want it as soon as possible and you assign say 30 people to it, you find it takes longer than the original six months.

This is called the "Mongolian horde" approach, and it is a very common mistake the big outfits continue to make. Fortunately you won't make this mistake, because you do not have a horde of troops to send storming into the battle, but don't think that more people will shorten the schedule. There is an optimum and least expensive way to do any job, and it takes a certain amount of time. However, if you wish to shorten the schedule, you can up to a point, but it will cost you in extra effort and increased costs. You get nothing for nothing. You can get your house painted in five days with four painters, that is (5 × 8 × 4) 160-man hours of work. You might get the job done in three days using nine painters, but that is (9 × 8 × 3) 216 man hours. However, there is no way you can possibly get the house painted in one hour using 160 painters. Somewhere between four people taking five days and 160 people working one hour the law of diminishing returns sets in and, at that point, each new person adds costs and actually does zero work. At this point added staff actually delays the work. It is up to you to know where this point is for every job you do.

Business school students have this drummed into them constantly, but most entrepreneurs have not been to business school and learn this lesson the hard way. This is especially hard when, for the first time, you have to try to handle a rapid and large increase in staff due to sudden growth. You grow from 20 to 100 people and find your production is not five times what it was, but only three times its former level, and you made the price on the wrong assumption. This mistake can indeed be a killer, can't it? I made that mistake, but I survived. I went to business school, and forgot what I was taught. I tried to do a job that would take one year for ten people to complete in six months with 20 people. It took nine months. Mea culpa! Due to fortunate circumstances, it was a research job on a "cost plus" basis, so we recovered the costs, but no fee for the extra effort. If that had been a "fixed price" job, it would have rocked our little outfit to its very foundations. Don't do what I did; you may not get a second chance.

ATTITUDES CHANGE AS YOU GROW

As you rapidly staff up, you won't get the extra loyalty, devotion, or effort from your new arrivals as from your old team, so don't expect it. They don't know you or how "great" you really are. It is just another job to these people, and why not? In fact, some of your old hands may even back off a bit when they see the new arrivals working at a slower pace, leaving right on time, or perhaps a bit early when no one is looking. The new employees receive the same, or worse, even a higher salary than the old hands receive. I know of no quicker and more effective way to destroy morale and create dissension than to pay new employees an equal or higher salary than the wages earned by your current staff. Don't think it will be a secret. Salaries always get out somehow, and when they do, what do you say to employees who have been with you for five or ten years when they are training a number of new hires and they learn that the newly hired workers outearn them? Watch for this! In your heady pursuit of new business and rapid growth, don't forget those faithful employees who worked for you for years when times were tough. They stood faithfully by when you needed them. That is what bonuses are for. Lay it on them right now! This is a happy combination of two sometimes divergent interests. It is morally right, and also good business. Never forget those who helped you when you needed them. It will help you grow even faster.

St. Peter was reviewing the life of a soul waiting to pass by into Heaven. St. Peter looked at the book on this fellow's life and the book was blank. No sins and no good acts either. Nothing to judge. St. Peter asked the man if he had not done some small thing during his life that helped someone, so he could tip the scales on the plus side and let him in. The man said: "Oh, yes, once ten years ago I gave a $2.00 donation in an office collection to help the poor." St. Peter was all set to admit him when St. Michael the Archangel came by, looked over St. Peter's shoulder at the judgment book and said, "Pete, give this guy his $2.00 back and tell him to go to Hell." Don't forget those who helped you get where you are.

CREEPING BUREAUCRACY FROM WITHIN

As many new people join your expanding staff, they don't know you, they don't know your style, or how you operate on your management plans and goals. It is natural then that they will draw upon their past experiences and apply these methods to the new job. This can be dangerous and harmful, especially if they come from very large companies or organizations that, by necessity, are bureaucratic. This is subtle and takes your constant attention to combat. It never goes away. Needless paperwork is generated. Reports and meetings start to proliferate. They even start having coordination meetings, for heaven's sake. Organizational "suboptimization" starts to set in. One group is under an ambitious manager who wants to "look better" than the other managers, which damages the organization as a whole because he or she looks no further than his or her own small area of responsibility. It shows up in increased overhead costs, internal politics and bickering, and a decrease in overall efficiency. They say things like, "This is how we did it where I worked before." They are not there anymore in body, but they are in spirit. It is difficult to combat, but it is even worse if you ignore it.

I tell my managers (weekly), "Don't give me big company practices until you first give me big company sales." A very bad combination is small company sales and big company bureaucratic procedures. The other way around is OK. You can also get bureaucratic if you want or must, but delay this for as long as possible. I would rather undermanage a $50 million contract than overmanage a $2 million job.

I was a manager on a former job for a big outfit. I looked forward to the first managers' meeting with the general manager. He held such meetings periodically. There were 15 managers, and I anxiously looked forward to the words of wisdom I was about to receive, so I could learn how to be a general manager. Boy, was I disappointed! The meeting lasted several hours, and we discussed reserved parking spaces, which secretaries get the new typewriters, and gossip and other trivia. I did not learn a thing, but I always went to future meetings. I was afraid not to show up.

A few months back at our managers' meeting, the subject of parking spaces came up. Since we were adding people to our staff, the parking lot was filling up. Some managers said the best spaces were filled and they had to park at the far end of the parking lot. First, I said I want the lot to fill up as quickly as possible. To me, this was a sign of expansion and growth, and not a problem at all. It was desirable. I told the managers that they can get the first parking spot right next to the front door. Their smiles faded from their faces, when I told them how. I told them to just drive right into them each and every morning. They replied that when they arrived they were all taken. Would I put up reserved signs for them? No, I would not! I just repeated that they could take any spot they wanted when they arrived in the morning. All they had to do was come to work early, when the lot was empty, and pick out any parking space they wanted. Democracy in action. The word of this meeting spread throughout the office, and I saw many more smiles than frowns from the staff. Things like this will do more good for morale than a big party, and it does not cost you one red cent.

As you grow, don't make the mistake of diverting your interests and activity on such nonproductive subjects. If you do, you will find costs going up and efficiency going down. You will be too tired and frustrated to work in the areas where your time, energy, and talents are required; i.e., more customers, financial planning, and new staff. Your job is the future, not the parking lot, typewriters, or furniture. Once again, the choice is yours.

In summary then, what are the typical growth mistakes that the small outfit can make?

1. No growth at all or a sudden decline.
2. Little or no thought or plans for the future.
3. Begging for work because you need it.
4. Trying to capitalize on friendship in lieu of performance.
5. Opulent display of your new found wealth and success.
6. Turning away new jobs because you don't like the work.
7. Pricing your work too low; the "buy in."
8. Expanding too fast.

9. Forgetting about or deferring profit.
10. Ignoring the law of diminishing returns.
11. Mongolian horde approach.
12. Change in corporate style from below, without your knowledge.
13. Forgetting those who helped put you where you are.
14. Getting mired down in nonessential trivia.

8

TEN STEPS TO DISASTROUS MERGERS

YOU SELL OUT JUST ONCE

NOW WE ARE getting back to the serious mistakes; one mistake here and you get no chance to recover. These mistakes are, in most cases, permanent and all you can do is cry. Perhaps mistakes made at this stage are even more serious and lasting than any mistake you may make up to this point. Why? Consider this situation. You and a few associates start up your new venture with high hopes and $50,000 in funding. You work your heads off, but 18 months later it is all over. It did not work. You go back to the old big outfit an older and wiser person. The small business is not the life for you. You gave it a shot and it did not work. Your ego is damaged a bit, but what the heck? You gave it your best shot and that is nothing to be ashamed of. Go lie down and bleed awhile and then rise up and fight again. Even if you never try again, at least you learned something, so it was not a total loss. You did not lose too much money anyway, did you?

That unhappy situation may be far preferable to this. You succeed and work hard for five to ten years and your company is a nice little prosperous going concern. Now some outfit approaches you to buy you out lock, stock and barrel, and you jump at it. Later you find it was not too good a deal. You get bounced within a year. Your old high salary and perks are suddenly gone. You were not too careful when you made the deal, and you find the acquiring company "aced you right out of the game" and you sold out at far too low a price. You worked your head off for many years and blew it at the crucial time and you get paid in stock that you can't sell for three to five years. During that period, your buyer goes under, so you lose it all, after all that hard work and success.

SYNERGISM IS LIKE THE PERFECT MARRIAGE

Permit me to fall back on the human versus the corporation comparison again. A merger is very similar to a wedding, only more difficult in two ways. First, there is no love between the participants, and, second, you have to learn to live with many new associates, not just one. The synergistic merger, in which each participant does better together than they would have separately, is about as common as the true 50/50 marriage which becomes more wonderful and happy as time goes on, and the lucky partners march hand in hand, growing in love and understanding, into their golden years. Do you know of any such perfect marriages? If you are part of one, you are a statistical anomaly, so count your blessings. The post-merger period of living with each other generally results in the owners of the acquired company having to do all of the adjusting. They bought you out, so why should they adjust to you? Before we get into the mistakes you can make in a merger, let's examine why and when any outfit would want to buy you out, what they are looking to accomplish, and why many want to sell out.

1. Purchaser buys you simply to make money.
2. Purchaser buys you on your next five year business plan, not on your past history.
3. Most companies seem to be acquired at the points where their annual sales reach $2.5 million or $8.0 million or around $12 million. Why? I don't know.
4. Owners of small businesses that are successful tend to outgrow their own businesses and they get restless and sell out of boredom, rather than just for the cash.
5. Purchasers want to see your assets in cash rather than in inventory, buildings, and equipment.

6. Lawyers and CPAs can be deal killers. They delay, mire you in minor details. They get paid whether or not you get what you want.
7. The buyer wants your gross operating profit, not your net, bottom-line profit that existed under your direction.
8. If you can get in one lump sum at least ten times your annual income from operating your small business, give the deal very serious consideration.
9. Seller sets the price; buyer sets the terms.

What are some common mistakes the seller can make in a merger deal?

1. Selling at too low a price.
2. Selling for the wrong reasons.
3. Selling to the wrong company.
4. Selling with a post-merger hold on you personally.
5. Selling with the purchase price dependent upon post-merger sales or profit.
6. Taking stock that can't be sold for a specific period of time.
7. Doing your own negotiations.
8. Selling out to another small company.
9. Taking too long to complete the deal.
10. Selling from a position of weakness.

SELLERS DON'T SURVIVE THE MERGER FOR VERY LONG

Before we take these mistakes on, one by one, please consider this. In most mergers, the officers and directors of the company that sold out generally want to leave or are "asked" to leave within 18 months after the merger takes place. Former high salaries and perks disappear quickly after the merger. You are not the boss anymore and you can no longer do it your way.

TEN STEPS TO DISASTROUS MERGERS

After many years of being free of supervision and direction, you suddenly get a boss again. He or she knows the "big bucks" you were given to sell out, and may resent it and take out his or her frustrations on you as a very wealthy subordinate. Your boss may be very severe and demanding on you personally. The "big shots" who bought you are at the corporate level and you won't work for them after the merger. You can no longer take a "business trip" just because you want to, and you can't buy things for your outfit on your own decisions. Think about these before, not after, you merge. It is too late then.

YOU SET THE PRICE

Selling out at too low a price is so obviously a major mistake, we don't have to dwell upon it. You will know it first, but it's done. A deal is a deal. Don't dwell on it. It can't be corrected. As said above, if you can get ten times (or more) than your current income up front, and the interest on it is equal to or higher than your current income, that is not a bad deal, is it? If you get the price you want, forget about what happens later. Take it and enjoy life. Only you as the seller can set the price. You have now one big decision to make, so make it and accept it. Also, it is a good idea to plan that what you get at the moment of the sale is all you are going to get. If you end up with more later, wonderful. If not, you won't be disappointed or upset. Be careful of post-merger holds on you.

SELLING FOR THE WRONG REASON

Some sell for the wrong reason, and later live to regret it. Some start out as co-owners, and the company takes off. One of the original group of owners works harder as the company grows, but the co-owners do not. He or she starts to think it was a mistake in having co-owners who do not do their share, or worse, cannot. He or she has plans to grow, but the co-owners are perfectly content with what exists and slow down or stop expansion plans completely. He or she becomes bored, listless, even disinterested in running an ever small outfit. He or she has time on his hands, and wants a bigger challenge.

There is no way to rearrange the ownership of the company stock. That is fixed so the next best way to sell out and get a fresh start with the new buyer. You are selling to try to compensate for a mistake made years earlier in the original formation of the company. Along comes a big outfit that offers you a glittering challenge to move forward with them into the big time. You jump at it and it does not work out. You are not as good as you thought you were and you find out the hard way. Everything will change after the merger and you will never know until after you do it, and you can't back out then. If you sell out for any reason other than the cash you get for your company, you are setting yourself up for disappointment at least and a severe change in lifestyle and income at worst.

Several years ago, we were approached by a West Coast outfit. The negotiations proceeded and I was invited, at their expense, to visit their West Coast home office. I met the president, and he told me that if I would agree to a lower initial selling price, he would set me up personally with a firm post-merger contract to "consult" for his outfit, and I did not have to even go to work. I asked what about my other stockholders. He said he would fire them after the merger, and don't worry about them. I am burdened with a conscience and I could not do it, even though the offer was most attractive and some of our minority stockholders are not. I felt my responsibility was to get the best price for all stockholders and job security for our employees, not just a good deal for me. That would be selling out for the wrong reason. Several years later, this "high flyer" outfit went into bankruptcy. Am I glad I did not bite on that deal!

Of course, you may do what you want with the company you own and the reasons that you want to sell are many and varied, i.e., age, illness, death of a key owner/worker, boredom, or arguing with co-owners. These factors can be more important than the highest price. The choice, of course, once again, is yours and you live with it, and it is permanent. Don't hurry it and jump at what appears to be a great deal for you. If anyone tells you that the offer must be accepted by some specific near term and date or no deal, be careful. You are being pressed to quickly accept the "opportunity of a lifetime." Marry in haste, repent at leisure. The same goes for any merger. Take your time, think it over. You only do this once.

THE HONEYMOON ENDS

Selling to the wrong company is just as bad as selling for the wrong reasons. If you plan to work for the acquiring company after the merger, it would be well to plan your post-merger activities before you sell out. Your company and you must fit into the buyer's scheme of things. If the buyer cannot or does not show you the post-merger operational plans for your outfit and where you fit into the plans, you may not like it at all after the sale. They may be buying you strictly to increase their earnings quickly, and not to expand your company's capabilities to further heights. They may be after only your list of current clients or contracts and plan to redirect the entire effort after they buy you out. You and your employees may not be the real reasons at all. If so, your rosy post-merger plans will go right out the window.

The most successful post-merger operations exist when you and your outfit have a clearly defined capability that you can see fits in with your buyer's plans. Strangely enough, many mergers succeed in which the buyer and seller have completely different lines of business. If the buyer has no or little capability in the type of business that you have, but wants to expand into that market, then you will be needed after the merger to assist in expanding into this area under their direction, with their assets to draw upon. If you sell to a bigger company in exactly the same line of business as yours, you may think this is great and you will all understand each other from day one. They may simply want your customers or staff to flush out their current staff. If so, goodbye! They won't need you that much, will they?

A friend sold his growing small outfit to a "biggie" in the same line of work. The original plan was to have the acquired company held as a wholly owned subsidiary with my friend as president, as he was for 15 years in running his own outfit. It all fell apart within six months. The new owners stripped him, step by step, of his key personnel for assignments to other projects of higher priority; his shrunken outfit was reduced in size to a department within the new company's organization structure. When a new reorganization drew him entirely within the new company's organization, he resigned and found the terms and conditions of the sale prohibited him from starting a new venture or working for any competition for a period of five years. He is home now, well paid, but pacing the floor and driving his wife up the wall. So, make sure you think it through and do not sell to the wrong company unless you plan to sell out and depart. Even in this case, you do have some responsibility not to leave your faithful employees leaderless in a new outfit. They helped you get what you got. Can you forget about them entirely? Once again, the choice is yours.

COUNT ONLY ON WHAT YOU GET UP FRONT

I have attended two seminars on mergers and acquisitions. One was conducted by a major business school and the other was conducted by an entrepreneur who travels around the country making a good living from his seminars. Naturally the tone and subject matter of the seminars were quite different. One was cerebral and academic and the other was entrepreneurial and pragmatic. There was one major point, however, that both seminars continually emphasized. It was that the seller should count only what is received at the moment of the sale. Any-post merger terms and conditions can cause you grief. It is a normal part of the deal that the seller agrees to some limitations on his business activity, if, for any reason, he or she resigns or is asked to leave the buyer's company. There is nothing wrong with this. I would do it, too. The buyer does not want to have you leave, start a new outfit, compete with them, hire back the best of your former staff, and create turmoil, trouble, and legal activity after they paid you well for your former company.

The post-merger agreement is negotiable and final. It is difficult and awkward for you to object to or try to loosen this post-merger hold before your sale takes place. You fear they might conclude that you plan to quickly depart and do just what the agreement is trying to prevent. It is similar to asking your intended spouse, before the wedding, to sign an agreement that if a divorce ever should occur, he or she waives any claims to the wealth and property that you bring to the marriage or stand to inherit later on. I read in the *Wall Street Journal* that the expanding divorce rate is causing many wealthy parents to insist upon these premarital agreements to protect their wealth from passing, via an unsuccessful marriage, outside of their family forever. Well, in a merger, there is no love involved, so it is suggested that you do not be afraid to address this problem and clear it up to your satisfaction.

Business is business and the odds are you will leave, one way or the other, within 18 months anyway. The purchase price may be so high that you may think you won't want to ever work again. You may feel that way when you see the check for the sale of your outfit, but a year or two later that may well change. You are 40 or 45 years old. Do you think you will be happy as a retiree? If so, then sign any agreement they put before you. If not, or if in any doubt, negotiate one that leaves you the opportunity to work elsewhere. The buyer will tell you the agreement is the standard one drawn up by their legal department, but, if they really want you and your outfit, it can be changed. Use your legal advisors and make sure the agreement does not tie you up completely forever or for so many years that it may as well be forever.

Play "what if." What if you do leave? What if you want to work again elsewhere? What if you get a chance later to own shares in another outfit? If so, what percent may you own? How? Where? What type of company? If you sell to a giant corporation, they may have interests in all sorts of companies, and if you try to start up another outfit in a completely new line of business than your former outfit, it still may be in competition with the buyer's company. Negotiate specifically the areas in which you will not compete, then all other areas are open to you. Negotiate for a specific period of time or a specific geographic area. Tie it down so you don't tie your hands.

YOU AREN'T THE BOSS ANY LONGER

Once again, be careful about payouts that are dependent upon future post-merger sales or profit. The buyer may tell you that you will be paid a percent of the purchase price on day one and the rest over a period of years, depending upon your succeeding in meeting your post-merger sales or profit plan. This can be another mistake that you cannot escape from later if, for reasons beyond your control, you are unable to meet the projections. Remember you come under the direction and control of the seller's management and they can control what your sales and profit will actually be. The buyer will not give you complete autonomous control over your company after the sale. Why would anyone buy your company and not take control over it? Wouldn't you?

Your new owners may direct you into new business areas in which you don't succeed. Why should you pay for following their direction when it does not work out? They may readjust your accounting system, for internal reasons, and actually reduce your reported profit. Why should you pay for that? They may make you commit your best people to major internal company projects; these people are no longer available for your expansion as they were before. The point is, the buyer, who now owns your old outfit, can do what he or she wants, when and where it pleases him or her.

Added payouts based on post-merger performance on your part can cause you severe disappointment, and you end up with far less than you thought you would get. One outfit who approached us gave me a formula that had post-merger payout as the basis of the sale. It was complicated, however, I figured out it was possible that I could have actually ended up owing them money if our post-merger sales dropped below the level at the point of the sale. I asked the buyer's lawyer if anyone ever signed such an agreement. I was advised that it was their standard merger procedure, and a number of small business owners had signed it and joined their organization. I suggested that anyone who would sign such an agreement should have his or her head examined. Beware of post-merger payouts. It is a risky and dangerous business. The people with whom you deal before the merger may be the soul of honesty and integrity, but others, not so encumbered morally, may take over your outfit later, and you never know who they will be. Also, remember, after the sale, you are no longer in absolute control. After the merger, just like after the marriage, things do change and you can't predict what these changes are until it is too late to change them.

CASH IS BEST

If you take stock in lieu of cash for payment, make sure the stock is negotiable by you. Cash is best, but you may be offered part cash and part stock or just stock. If you sell to a giant corporation, the number of shares you own may be so small that whether or not you sell them, it will not make the price drop. However, if you sell out to another small company, even though your stock is sellable, if you try to sell off a large block at one time, it may drastically affect the price and make your new owner very upset with you.

Taking unregistered stock is dangerous as well. It is not negotiable. Get competent legal advice before you accept anything like this. I am not up on all of the details about unregistered stock, but I am a bottom-line man. All I know is you have limitations on the resale of this stock and the explanations given to me did not satisfy me that it was all that good a deal. If you take stock up front, and, for any reason, they place limitations on you so you cannot sell it when and where you like, then it is to your advantage to negotiate a "floor" for the price of the stock. The "floor" fixes a minimum price for your stock and if the market price for your stock ever drops below the "floor," you get the difference from your buyer in cash. It is sort of a stock option in reverse. There is even some danger here. If your buyer goes bankrupt and has no funds to pay you, what then? Remember, in any bankruptcy, the owners get paid last. You could have the cash put in escrow beyond the reach of your buyer, but this gets complicated and very good legal services are needed to protect your interests. Also, the buyer may not want to tie up the cash in such a deal. Why not just pay you with it up front?

DON'T YOU BELIEVE IT

If the buyer tells you the stock you get will greatly appreciate in price in the coming years, so that you will be better off taking stock in lieu of cash, I suggest you tell them this. If they believe what they are telling you, let them give you cash and let them keep their own stock and they will benefit as the stock appreciates, as they are telling you it will. If they really believe what they are telling you, they would much prefer to give you cash up front. If they don't believe what they are saying, or they are not sure, let them take the risk, not you, because after you sell, they are in charge, not you. Let them win or lose on their own management abilities, not yours.

A good way to think about this is to consider your company as a car and someone wants to buy your car for X dollars and then hire you to be their chauffeur and drive the car where they tell you to go. Fine! You got X dollars to sell the car as one final and complete deal. You get Y dollars to be the chauffeur, and if, for any reason, later you get into an accident and damage the car, they can adjust or stop paying you the Y dollars, but you keep the X dollars no matter what happens later. Let them negotiate post-merger incentives for you in the same way as they do for their current executives with bonuses, perks, and stock options, but not by adjusting, up or down, the X dollars you get for selling your company on day one.

HIRE PROFESSIONAL NEGOTIATORS

Don't do your own negotiations. This is a job for the professionals. The buyer is, in all probability, a bigger outfit than you and they have a team of professional negotiators who buy companies and they know their business. You don't, so hire the professionals to represent you. When anyone is buying anything—i.e., a house, a car, or any major purchase—it is natural for the buyer to look for things to criticize just to lower the price. If you are present and you listen to the buyer's team publicly criticize some portion of your pride and joy, you will get defensive and emotional, impairing your ability to negotiate.

Also, during the negotiations, the individual from the buyer's organization who actually signs the final deal will not be present. If you, as the owner and the one who signs for your company, are always present, you may say or do something, during the negotiations, that binds your company. A verbal consent or quick agreement may be final, and you can't back off later. At the merger seminar that I attended, the lecturer warned specifically against owner participation in the negotiations. He said one ploy the buyers sometimes use is, in the midst of the push and shove going on, the seller is quietly drawn away and offered a price for a quick sale to end all of the discussion. This works sometimes in the heat of the moment, but the handshake binds the deal on your part, but can be later adjusted by the seller who can claim his agent had no authority to make the deal.

Paid professionals who represent you can negotiate the very important details for you—i.e., payout plan, cash versus stock, and post-merger work agreements—without your personally being present and appearing too grasping or too mercenary. Do it the way the buyer does. Let your representatives fight the battle. You, like the general, remain at headquarters and issue the orders, and you only come to the game for the formal signing of the merger agreement. Being not present does not mean that you are not in control. On the contrary, it means you are very much in charge, so long as your representatives follow your instructions and do not exceed their authority or get you bogged down in side issues. You won't get everything you want exactly as you want it, so leave the haggling and trade off details to your hired representatives just as the buyer does.

SELL TO THE 'BIGGIES'

There is some danger and risk if you sell out to another company that is not too much bigger than you are. Even though the buyer may be creating a new corporate empire by acquiring a collection of various small companies to implement his or her master plan, the end result may be disaster. Here are some things to watch out for:

1. You are very likely going to get a lower price than from a big buyer because the small buyer is giving out his or her own cash or stock. The big buyers are not.
2. You are much less likely to receive cash. Most expanding small outfits are cash short. They use stock.
3. If you accept stock in payment, it is very likely not going to be negotiable by you at your choice.
4. The possibility of later, sudden bankruptcy is there. High fliers do crash you know. I have seen outfits start out fast, grow rapidly, and burst in mid-air.

Post-merger operations are, in general, more difficult with the small company buyout than with the "big boys." The large outfit has done it before and has experiences with living together with other companies after the honeymoon is over. A company president, who paid you several million dollars or its equivalent in stock, is naturally going to be a much more demanding boss than some big company general manager, who is now your boss, but paid nothing of his or her own personal assets to acquire you. He or she will be much more objective and reasonable if things don't go according to the post-merger plans. They seldom do, you know.

DON'T DRAG IT OUT

Good mergers happen fast. Whether you contact the buyer or the buyer contacts you, if it does not happen quickly, it probably won't happen at all. In the good merger, you can do all the analysis and studies you like, however if the "chemistry" or mutual attraction is not present, the merger won't happen. This "chemistry" has to happen between two people, you and the individual in the buyer's outfit who wants to buy your outfit. Like love, you cannot define it to anyone who has never experienced it. You tell them, "You'll just know when it happens.

You will know when the chemistry is there and when it is not, because you won't feel or experience it." It is also known as being on the same wavelength. Your natural and intuitive decisions and judgments just coincide with the other person's and you both know it. I have it with one of our co-owners, and it is a pleasure for us to work with each other. I do not have it with other stockholders, and it is not so pleasant. This chemistry must exist for the good merger to happen and be successful afterward. Without it, negotiations drag on and on and generally die out.

Rumors of an impending sale of your outfit will get out. They always do, and they can be very disturbing to your employees and rightly so. So, if you start the "romance" between you and a buyer, you'd better "get married" within a few months or break it off. Set a mutual date to prepare and sign a letter of intent with the price stated, subject to any final negotiations and conditions the buyer may set. Then settle these conditions, one by one, within a month or two. If you can't, and it drags on, stop it because, in most cases, one side or the other is having second thoughts, due to unsatisfactory detailed negotiations. Since you, rather than the buyer, stand to lose the most by protracted and fruitless negotiations, it is up to you to end it. If you tell the buyer you must settle it, one way or the other by a certain date, you will find out right then and there if they want you. They will say "yes" or "no," and then you know. What is a reasonable time period from start to finish? There is no real answer to that, but six to nine months seems plenty of time if it is ever going to happen.

SELL FROM STRENGTH

The best time to sell your company is when it is strong, vigorous, and expanding. Someone approaches you, because they like your track record, your company reputation, you personally, your abilities, your staff, your clients, or whatever. At these times, you will get your best price. However, some try to sell when things are going wrong; they want to escape with what they can get before the boat sinks.

Internal bickering among the owners has become a permanent way of life and you just can't stand it any longer. So you must want out. Sales are off and you may lose your biggest customer in six months, and no one knows it yet but you. You think you'd better get what you can before the balloon bursts. A principal owner dies and his estate is causing you severe company problems over the sale and distribution of the decedent's stock. Illness of key owners results in serious problems.

For whatever reason, if you try to sell out from a position of weakness, you will pay for it. Corporate bargain hunters are always on the lookout for a nice small company with growth potential that is poorly managed, for whatever reason. They may rush in and offer you a quick way out of your immediate dilemma. Your emotions are involved. I don't know what your batting average is when you make decisions under emotional stress, but mine is very low. I suspect yours is too. I do not mean I never use my emotions or intuition in making judgments, but I never let them control me in business. If I get angry, I go home. If I am upset, I wait until I calm down. Don't rush into a quick sale under stress. It generally does not pay off. You will get a very low price.

DON'T TRY TO HIDE ANYTHING

If you approach buyers, the first thing they will ask you is, "Why do you want to sell?" If your reason is to escape from an unpleasant or difficult situation, it probably won't happen at all. Even if it does, you depress the selling price greatly. Still some make the mistake of selling for emotional reasons, or when their company is going through a downward slide or is in some turmoil. You won't be able to hide or keep your real reason for selling a secret from the buyers. They will closely review your company situation and they will find out. If you try to mislead them, either they will immediately back out, or they will buy you at their price and send you packing. No one wants to bring anyone into their organization knowing, in advance, that they lie, twist the truth, or misrepresent themselves.

Some fortunes have been made by wise investors who bought out a company that was on the rocks due to poor management, but, in those cases, the sellers did not do too well. They took what they could get.

I am not saying not to sell if you are in a position of weakness, no indeed. Half a loaf is better than none, but remember if you are selling from a position of weakness, you will be very, very lucky to get even half a loaf. You will find very little sentiment exists when the bargain hunting tigers are on the prowl, and you happen by when they are hungry and you are weak.

A few entrepreneurs have become instant millionaires from a sale of their company at the right time, to the right buyer, but many others have not done too well. A mistake made in a merger is a one of a kind error. You do not get a second chance to recover and to try again with your company. It is permanent! You can write off years of effort if you do not do it well.

In summary then, what are some of the mistakes to watch out for if and when you consider a merger?

1. Selling at too low a price.
2. Selling for the wrong reason.
3. Selling to the wrong company.
4. Selling with a post-merger hold on you.
5. Selling with the purchase price dependent upon post-merger sales or profit.
6. Accepting payment in stock that you cannot sell.
7. Doing your own negotiations.
8. Selling to another small company.
9. Taking too long to complete a deal.
10. Selling from a position of weakness.

DO IT RIGHT THE FIRST TIME

When, after years of time, effort, and expense, you get your chance to merge, "don't make the same mistake once." Do it right and good luck to you. Now it all pays off for you, as you hoped and planned it would, and at a nice low capital gains tax rate as well. Now go and enjoy life, if your spouse can stand you around the house all day long. If not, go buy two houses. Why not? Now you can afford them.

9
HOW TO GO PUBLIC WITH STYLE

YOUR SMALL BUSINESS venture comes of age when you "go public." That is, you sell shares of your company on the stock market, or "over the counter," as it is called. Here is another way, besides the good merger, for you to become an instant millionaire, on paper at least. Once again, here we enter an area in which, if you do it well, the payoff can be tremendous. However, if a serious mistake occurs, your years of time and effort are quickly lost. Generally the hope or dream of most small business entrepreneurs is to see their companies' stock bought and sold on the open market with the price there for all to see. The entrepreneur holds 30 to 40 percent of the company's stock that is now worth millions. Some of the mistakes made in going public can be later corrected. All are not completely irreversible, but they are very expensive lessons. It is best to avoid all the mistakes that you can in any area, but especially so in the areas of mergers and going public.

GET THE BEST

You are entering an area in which you very likely have little or no experience or expertise, and you have to put your company in the hands of a broker and lawyer. If they do not do a good job in taking you public, you pay a heavy price. The broker and lawyer are paid up front, no matter what happens to you or to your fine company. I suggest caution in choosing the brokers to take you public. The big brokerage firms probably won't take you public. Most, if not all, have a minimum size for any stock deal that they will handle and that, most likely, will be far above the market value of your company at the time. Before you start down this road, it is well for you to talk to bankers and lawyers who handle what are called "initial offerings." Also, if you know anyone who has gone public, talk with them and listen up. He or she may save you from a serious and costly mistake.

What are some of the mistakes that you can make in going public?

1. Going public too soon.
2. Setting too low a price for your first offering.
3. Going public at the wrong time.
4. Selling too much stock.
5. Underestimating the initial total expenses.
6. Writing a poor prospectus.
7. Trading on insider information.
8. Being unprepared for internal company changes.
9. Ignoring external factors that can affect the price of your stock.
10. Trying to sell off personal shares later.

DON'T GO PUBLIC TOO SOON

Some, in their haste to go public, do so too soon in their development cycle. When future sales and profit do not materialize, the public or the brokers lose interest in your outfit and it takes many years to reverse the trend of your stock prices. Those who buy stock in new ventures are taking a big gamble due to the high failure rate of small ventures. They are buying your stock hoping to see a quick and steady increase in sales and profit, so their stock in your company will appreciate in value quickly. You are not what is called "blue chip stock," not by a long shot. The blue-chip stocks are the big and reputable firms who have been in business for years and who in all probability will survive, barring a major economic upheaval. People will take a lower growth rate with the blue chips, but not from a high-risk stock. If your company performance does not very quickly show dramatic change for the better with the cash you received from your initial sale of stock, you many never recover. Some have gone public, survived, and later decided to buy back the public stock and become a closely held corporation again. What a costly error to make and end up back where you started. Don't rush into it. It is difficult to reverse the process once you do it, but not impossible. On a scale of one to ten, I would rate an error in going public too soon as an eight. Not deadly, but very serious.

YOU'RE WORTH WHAT YOU GET

Setting too low a price on your initial sale is a common mistake. You have no way to judge your worth, so other "experts" will do it for you. You give up a large percentage of your ownership in your company for what later proves to be far too low a price. It does not matter if you later fail, because 1 percent or 50 percent of nothing is nothing, but if you really take off, you may look back with regret on the low price you received for 30 to 40 percent of your company's stock for what is now a very prosperous and growing venture. The stock you sold for $2.00 a share is now up to $10.00 a share, due to your efforts as president or as a senior officer in your now publicly traded company. You may need the funds received for expansion and growth, but there are other ways to get funds. Once you sell or give away any shares in your enterprise, they are gone, unless you can buy them back later.

I made the mistake of a premature distribution of stock in 1964 for far too low a price, and 20 years later, that decision still haunts me. Was I ever stupid! Kindly friends and associates said I was inexperienced and too generous, but I had no older mentor to put a hand on my shoulder and say, "Hold it, Bill, do you realize what you are doing?" As the French say, "It was worse than a crime, it was a blunder." Don't you do it! In one case, we had to buy back a substantial number of shares from one of the recipients of this premature stock distribution at about 30 times what he had paid for it. Whenever I get on my "high horse" and start to think I am pretty good, all I have to do is think about what I did at the start. I mumble "stupid" to myself and I become properly humble again (for a few days).

TIME IS OF THE ESSENCE

Coming to the market to sell your stock at the wrong time can prove to be a bad mistake. During a recession, the market goes down and pessimism prevails. The general trend is downward, so will your stock tend to follow the market trends? Why not? Are you really that special? You may buck the trend, but it is more difficult to swim upstream than down, no matter how strong a swimmer you are. It takes quite a few months to get ready to sell your stock, and if during that period general business conditions go bad, you may have to pull up short and stop or wait. This is costly in time, effort, and money. If you proceed anyway, you may not be able to sell all of your first offering. This is not only bad news financially, it can be downright embarrassing to your corporate public image. You shout to the business world, "Here I come!" and everybody yawns and ignores you. Being in the right place at the right time is, in part, chance or luck, but you have to do something about it and that is not luck. Timing is important in anything in life, and especially so when you choose to go public.

DON'T LOSE CONTROL

Selling off too large a share of your company not only brings you in too small an amount of money for the amount sold, but opens up another unpleasant possibility. If, for any reason, you release a majority of shares to public offering, you have no control over who buys them. What can happen if a small group of investors buys up all or most of these shares because they like your outfit's growth and potential? At first you are pleased, because as they buy up the shares, the price per share rises. It is a seller's market for a while, and it all looks good. However, the shares are being acquired by a small group of investors who will at the next annual stockholders' meeting assert their ownership position by voting their shares as a block. They can get seats on your board of directors, or worse, take control of your company. Don't laugh, it has happened.

This outside group could approach one of your company's officers and with these shares, plus their own, outvote you. What happens to you then? One mistake, and it is "flowers for the widow" again. Many entrepreneurs have been dumped from their own companies in this way. In fact, it is not at all uncommon, and it usually happens in the midst of growth, expansion, and general corporate prosperity. That is just the time someone will want to take over, isn't it? Who wants to take over when things are going poorly? In that case, they won't even buy your stock in the first place, or if they do, they will wait until your company is on the road upward.

What a rude shock awaits any founding entrepreneur, who is suddenly and legally pushed aside from his or her own outfit, because the majority stockholders want new leadership. They can do it and they may well be correct. It may be time for someone else to take over, but do you want a say in this major decision for you and your company, or do you want to let others do it for you? Once again, the choice is yours; selling off too large a piece of your outfit makes this a real possibility or even a good probability.

In a recent local court case, the founder of a well-established company was dismissed by outside majority stockholders from his own company. The company bears his name. He left and started up another outfit and tried to get his name back from his old outfit. He lost. He can't even use his own name for his new company. Be careful here. You'd better know exactly what you are doing or you can even end up losing your name. The original founder of a company tends to get put aside as the "baby" grows up. Selling off large shares of your growing company only increases the probability that it will happen to you sooner rather than later. I have a quick quiz for you to prove my point. Most of us readily associate the name Sloan with General Motors. Who founded General Motors? If you came up

HOW TO GO PUBLIC WITH STYLE 145

with the name Durant, you get A+ for your knowledge of corporate history. Be careful how you divert yourself of your company stock.

WATCH THOSE EXPENSES

Going public is expensive. Your brokerage house will charge you an arm and a leg for their services. Sometimes they even demand shares in your company at very low prices for them to take you public. You may have to do this because you do not have enough cash to pay them up front. I suppose if they own shares in your now publicly owned stock, they may continue helping you grow in order to benefit from the increased value of your stock on the open market. But, they now own stock in and have voting rights in your company. Do you want this to happen?

Many more forms, reports, and procedures must be made out and followed. You have to publish an annual report. Government regulations and procedures require your time, your lawyer's time, and your CPA's time. The cost quickly adds up. These are permanent costs that will occur each and every year from now on, over and above the high one-time initial expense that you pay to sell your first offering to the public. The costs can easily go well into six figures. Are you ready to pay for his new and fixed expense? None of this helps you find new clients, lower your costs, or increase your profits. There is another expense over and above just the financial costs: the expense in time and energy on your part. You now have several thousand (you hope) stockholders. When any of them call up and want to talk to you about how their company is doing, you'd better speak to them or hire (more costs) someone to always be ready when they call. You want stockholder support at the annual meeting, don't you? Shut off someone or ignore the "pest" with ten shares who calls every week, and you will hear from them loud and clear at the annual meeting. Do you really need this yet? You may even retain majority ownership, but minority rights exist and they can affect you.

Also, your salary, perks, and business expenses will become public knowledge. Your employees will find out everything, because some will buy stock in your venture to get a copy of your annual report. Now you work for them, too. If you are still quite small, with some employees owning shares in your venture, what do you do if they collectively vote their shares as a bloc and want representation on your board of directors? Do you want this now? When you are big enough, it doesn't matter that much. The expenses are trivial in comparison with your total sales. However, if you are not that big and these expenses in money and time bear down on you, it is too late to change them. You'd better figure out the total price to you before you do it.

PREPARING A PROSPECTUS

To go public, you have to prepare a prospectus that announces what you are going to do with the money you receive from those who buy the stock. This is required by law, to protect the public. Before the SEC had such laws, the raping and pillaging that went on made Ivan the Terrible look like a boy scout at a church picnic. You had better know what you are doing when you prepare and issue this prospectus. One mistake here and you can get arrested. This is a job for the professionals and it is expensive. Don't cut costs here. If you do, it is about as cost effective as trying to remove your own appendix to save the surgeon's fee. You find the mortician costs your estate even more than you "save." Get the best and pay for it. Careful selection of your legal staff is vital. Your corporate lawyer is probably not qualified for this special task.

After you sell your stock, you must spend the funds received in the way you stated in your prospectus. If, for any reason, you depart from this plan, you open yourself up to lawsuits by any stockholder, the SEC, or both. Also, the corporate shield may not protect you from personal financial losses either. Recent trends indicate that corporate officers can be held personally liable for mistakes they make in handling corporate funds of a company that is owned in part by the general public. If it can be later proven to the satisfaction of a judge or jury that you did

HOW TO GO PUBLIC WITH STYLE

not "exercise due diligence" or "reasonable prudence" in your business judgments, you can be sued personally. Not following your prospectus is not only bad business judgment, is it illegal.

Some judges and juries tend to favor the small stockholder in such lawsuits. Recently I read about a company president of a small business who told several of his employees that the price for the company stock in the market was far too low. New contracts and future business situations would soon drive the stock up in price. Some of his employees went out and bought some shares. The price increase did not follow. In fact, the stock later decreased in price. These people sold their stock at a loss and got a lawyer who used the president to retrieve their loss. Somehow they were able to prove in court that the employees felt "compelled" to buy the stock when the president spoke to them. They said they were afraid they would be somehow punished if they did not do what the president said. He claimed he was in no way forcing anyone to do anything. He was merely expressing his opinion about future business activity that did not materialize. In any case, he lost and had to pay back personally the losses suffered by his obedient employees.

You cannot sell stock in a prospectus by predicting any growth profit that you think will follow. You can only state what you plan to do with the money received, and you had better do exactly that with the funds. You cannot arbitrarily shift gears after you get the funds even if the opportunity of a lifetime presents itself. You can take the risk if you want. If it pays off handsomely, you will be praised for your good leadership since the stock went up in price, but if it does not, stand by for trouble.

Give very careful thought to what goes into your prospectus. It ties your hands legally and morally on how you spend these funds later on. A mistake made here is a ten on the scale, because it can put you in court.

FOLLOW THE RULES

Trading on insider information is another very serious mistake you may make in your ignorance that you are doing anything wrong. Once again, this mistake is a "ten" because it is illegal. As president, a corporate officer, or a senior person within your company, your job is to do your best for those who buy and own shares in your company. The captain of a ship does not jump into the first lifeboat when the ship springs a leak, leaving the passengers and crew to take care of themselves. The captain is supposed to be the last one off, or even better, go down with the ship in good navy tradition. This captain gets a statue and posthumous awards and is honored forever more.

In running your small outfit, you become aware of all things, good or bad, that are about to happen to your company. You are going to sign a new contract tomorrow that will double your sales over the next year or two. When the word hits the street, your stock will rise. If you think you can call your broker and buy a few thousand shares of your company's stock over the counter and then release the good word, think again my friend. You "reason" that you bought the stock that was available for sale just as in any normal stock transaction. Others think differently. They think you used your inside information to your personal advantage to the loss of current stockholders who were depending upon you to represent them in their best interests. Clearly you did not do this. You looked out for Number One at their expense. You suddenly are informed that your biggest client will not review your contract that will run out in 90 days. No one knows it but you. So, you call your broker to sell what shares you have before the word gets out and the price drops. You let it drop and then buy back the shares for half the price you got two months earlier. Don't try that one either. You traded on inside information at the stockholders' expense.

You could buy or sell it through a third party and give them a fee to represent me. Don't try that one either. It is just as illegal as the above situations. You may be a millionaire on paper, but be careful as to how to sell off your shares later. You must do it openly, publicly, and by following all the SEC rules and regulations.

It can be a great temptation when you are in possession of information that you know will directly affect the price of your company's stock to call a friend or relative and advise them to buy or sell their stock in your enterprise, but that is illegal. Ignorance of the law is no excuse and some well-intentioned actions on your part, even if not in your own self interest, to help out a friend or relative, can crash down on you like a lightning bolt. It is all over for you, or you can end up in court as the defendant. That is hardly a way to leave your company, is it?

STAND BY FOR MORE CHANGES

After going public, your internal company operations will change. They will become more formal and more bureaucratic. You had better plan for this change, because it will occur either from the top down or from the bottom up. You will have to conform to various new government regulations. You will have to hold regular, formal board of directors' meetings. You will have to document what you do, why, and when. A written audit trail to justify your actions will be necessary. You never know when or where these "requests" will come in. A stockholder writes to ask why you got a 10 percent pay raise this year, while the stock price did not increase. You skipped a dividend payment. Why?

You are no longer as free as you once were to "wheel and deal" as you think best. You can no longer commit company funds on some "intuitive" decisions that you reached. You can, I suppose, but your written report, on this decision, must contain "valid" business reasons to justify your actions, so you have to write up something that "looks good" to others. You no longer own it all. You have owners who are protected by many laws and procedures that restrict your former freedom of activity to suddenly change course, go into an entirely new line of work, or advance funds to pursue a target that appears good to you, but is not in your business plan or your annual report. The tendency now is to become conservative and plan not to lose, rather than take risks to win.

What we call "diaper management" sets in. You cover your own bottom first, before you do anything else. You let opportunities pass unchallenged because there is risk if you lose, but not that much for you to gain, personally, if you succeed. The old owners cannot meet any longer and informally vote each other big bonuses, new cars, or other perks. It must be according to plan and be acceptable to your stockholders. Even some of your old first team of loyal employees, who liked the way it was in the old days, may not like the new, formal, and businesslike operations. You may not like it either; but it has to change, and formats, procedures, and forms start to become as important as your substance.

Are you ready for all these changes after you "go public"? If not, the mistakes you make are not all fatal, in themselves, but they are irritants, and may force you to change your old management style. The new styles and procedures may not be to your liking, and thus will reduce your daily on-the-job performance.

OTHER THINGS AFFECT YOUR STOCK

External factors will affect the price of your stock in the market. General economic conditions, the illness or death of a public person, rumors about future trends of business in general or yours in particular, prime interest rate fluctuations, and other factors in the macroeconomic sphere cause the entire market to rise or fall. Your individual company performance is important, perhaps the most important factor, but is only one of the factors that will affect the rise or fall of its price. It can be very disheartening for a small business that is doing well when its stock does not move upward due to a general malaise that affects the entire economic community. So called "glamour stocks" enter the market, are bought, and sold at very high price–earning ratios. Suddenly the "bloom is off the rose," you are earning more profit than ever, but the interest in your industry has passed on to another area. The industry price–earnings ratio for companies like yours declines so, increased profits or not, the price for your stock decreases as you grow and produce more profit.

Most investors who buy into small ventures going public for the first time are not looking for immediate dividends; they

HOW TO GO PUBLIC WITH STYLE

want growth in the value of the stock for capital gains later. If you start issuing good dividends too early, two things can happen. First, it won't make your stock go up very fast or in proportion to the dividends paid. In fact, some investors would prefer to see you retain your profits for greater company growth. Next, high dividends will attract some investors who are looking for regular income to support themselves. They are not interested in rapid growth, because that is not what they want. Now, if for any reason, you later reduce or skip a dividend to spend the funds on new business growth, even if you grow, the "dividend investors" may complain or sell off their stock in large numbers to put their money where they will get dividends.

So, be ready for outside forces over which you have absolutely no control to affect the price of your stock, so you can explain it all to someone with ten shares who calls up to find out why your stock dropped along with the rest of the market. These ten-share owners know nothing about the big picture. All they know is your stock decreased in price by 25 percent last week. What do you tell them? Also, remember, these external factors affect the price of the stock that you own as well. Consider this before you go public. It is not all beer and skittles. The big outfits can wait out economic fluctuations, but can you?

STOCK ISN'T ALWAYS MONEY

Now we get to the biggie! You are a millionaire on paper and you want to sell off some or all of your stock in your venture. Let's say you own 200,000 shares in the company with 800,000 shares owned by the public at $10 per share. The market value of your company is simple to compute; $10 per share times 1 million shares means $10 million. So, if you sell your 200,000 shares, you will get $2 million, right? Wrong! You very likely won't get that much. Here is why.

A sudden and large block of your stock up for sale will decrease the price because there may not be enough buyers who want that much stock. That much of a transaction or activity in your stock movement triggers immediate interest from investors.

What is going on? Why is this big block of stock up for sale? The investors or the brokers find out the company president is selling off his or her entire ownership in the company. They think, "I had better sell my stock too before it goes down even further. If the top person is selling out, why should I hold my stock? He or she must know something that I don't know." A flood of sell orders come in and the $10 per share quickly drops to $5 per share or even lower.

There was absolutely nothing wrong with your company. Things are going fine. You just wanted to retire and let others take over and expand the company. Your decision to sell it all at once was a mistake and it cost you $1 million on the way out. Later, everyone calms down, the stock returns to its $10 per share value with you gone, and those who bought your stock are very pleased. They doubled their money in six months at your expense. I would rate that mistake as an 11 on the error scale, wouldn't you?

You will have to dispose of your stock in an orderly and predictable way that everyone knows about, understands, and accepts. Everyone knows that you will sell the stock sooner or later. What good does it do locked in a safe deposit box? It is an investment, and sooner or later you cash it in. It is best that you announce it, well in advance, before you try to sell off your stock. Do not sell it in one lump sum. You may have to sell off in phases, a little at a time. The brokers call this procedure an "orderly market." Your sale's impact on the general trading of your company's stock is not greatly noticed or not great enough to decrease the price for all stockholders. If you hold on to it until you die before selling it, you made two mistakes.

- You don't benefit at all from your years of effort.
- The IRS may demand the inheritance taxes at a price per share before your estate is forced to sell it off. The price your estate recovers may be well below the price the IRS sets on your estate.

If you are the business person that I think you are, you wouldn't be too happy looking down from above, watching your loved ones paying taxes at the rate of $10 per share when your stock is selling for $5 per share. Your heirs would question you business acumen for leaving them in such a mess.

Plan ahead when to sell your shares. Set a date, an age, stock price, date of retirement, or any other valid reason for it. When the time comes, you can postpone it if you want, or sell the stock at a slower rate than planned. No one can make you adhere to your original plan. It gives you the option to sell or not at the future date, but if you have no plan and it suddenly happens, you know what can happen. That is another mistake that is an "11."

PLAN GOING PUBLIC

So, going public is a good thing to do, but it must be carefully planned and well executed, because the mistakes, if not all killers, are all very expensive and difficult to reverse or to correct later on.

The most irritating mistakes among those who have gone public are going public too soon, receiving too little for the initial offering, and experiencing difficulty in disposing of their personal shares. So, learn from their mistakes. Experience is, of course, the best teacher, but the tuition for the lessons to be learned from your mistakes made in going public can be very, very high, even in the millions.

You will get little sympathy from others when you complain you ended up only with $800,000 which should have been $2 million, because you made a few "going public mistakes." They will think you are bragging when you really are not. It is a shame if you do all the difficult work well, survive the early years, fight the odds, and get your outfit into a position to go public and then make your first big mistake. This is your chance. Now is the time to make it pay off for all of your years of time and effort. We are all human, and we all do make mistakes, but if you have to make mistakes, be selective and do not make any when you go public. Make them elsewhere, if you must, where they don't hurt you so much.

10

LEARNING FROM MISTAKES, WATCHING FOR LUCK

THIS BOOK IS about mistakes, and I suppose more negative errors than positive. I regret the necessity of discussing mistakes for nine chapters without making some attempt to be a bit more positive. As said earlier, there are many kinds of mistakes one can make in his or her personal and professional lives. There are mistakes and there are big mistakes. If you go on a blind date and spend a dull, boring evening with a "creep," that is a mistake. If you get married and then find out your spouse is a "creep," that is a big mistake. If you take a job somewhere, and it does not work out, that is a mistake. If you spend your life's savings to start a business, borrow $100,000 with your home as security, and then fail, that is a big mistake. However, big or small, the only redeeming factor from making a mistake is you can learn something from it.

MISTAKES ARE EXCELLENT TEACHERS

In school when you took a test and received a grade of 100 percent, what did you learn from taking the test? Nothing! You knew it all and your answers were perfect. This is fine for your grade point average and super for your ego, but did you learn anything by taking the test? No, you did not. However, if you got a grade of 90 percent, and you went back to your instructor to find out why you missed the last question and lost 10 percent, then you learned something.

I drove to my son's school to deliver some money he needed, and I met a friend of his. This young man was from Geneva. I asked him what was his major in school, and he said French. His native language was French. Why was he coming all the way to the United States to go to school to study French? He said it was easy and he got all A's and first honors on the Dean's list. I said I thought he was making a big mistake and he should study things he does not know anything about, so he could learn something. He replied by saying I sounded just like his father, so I shut up and drove him home. He will learn about his mistake, later, when he goes looking for a job; unless, of course, he has wealthy parents, in which case it won't matter at all. In fact, in this case, it would not be a mistake. Mistakes do have one good point: they teach you things, the hard way.

TEACH YOURSELF

There are three ways to learn anything. First, and the best way, is to be so brilliant that you can teach yourself anything. The child prodigy, who, at four years of age, climbs up on a piano stool, reaches out, and starts playing the piano well and just gets better and better as time goes on; the person who can learn a foreign language by listening to tape recordings one time and never forgetting; the student who reads through a book on advanced mathematics and understands it all; these are rare and gifted individuals, who are capable of teaching themselves. There are not enough of them around to concern yourself about, because it is most likely you will never encounter one directly in your working career. It is just as well. They usually are very difficult people to be near and even more difficult to understand and work with. They are out on a cloud all by themselves; we tend not to like them because we feel inferior just being around them.

LEARN FROM OTHERS

Another way to learn is by letting others teach you or by books, in which you listen, read, think, and benefit from the experience and guidance of others and the information they can bring to your attention. This is a very good way for most of us to learn. It is called education. You allow yourself to benefit yourself by learning from the mistakes others have made ahead of you. Since most of us are not one of those rare individuals who can teach themselves all they have to know, we should learn from others.

LEARN BY EXPERIENCE (THE HARD WAY)

Now we get to the third method. You learn by your own experiences and mistakes. There is no question that experience is the best teacher, but it is painful, unforgiving, and very expensive. Psychologists estimate that 85 percent of us learn best by experience. If that is the way it is, OK, but I suggest you try to be in that 15 percent who do not have to go through the painful process of learning by their own mistakes. In the small business area, the price you pay to learn your lessons may be the death of your nice small company. That is a heavy price to pay for a mistake or two, isn't it?

THE REPEATERS

However, there is even a worse situation in dealing with mistakes. They are called the repeaters. These unfortunate individuals do not learn from their own mistakes so they make the same mistakes or very similar mistakes over and over again. They never seem to learn. Why? Beats me, but some of us are this way. The only benefit that can possibly be gained from making a mistake is to learn from it, but you have to let yourself learn. If you refuse to admit it was your error, or you try to assign the blame to someone else, or use some other ego-saving device, then stand by for a repeat performance. You are a repeater.

The most successful people I know have made many mistakes and the stories they will tell you about their errors are often very amusing, because they are not afraid to admit to their human faults. However, these people never repeat the mistake. Once is enough! Now, at the other end of the line, I know some

LEARNING FROM MISTAKES

who are not very successful, but they will tell you they don't make many mistakes. If you try to point out any of their mistakes, they are ready to argue that it was not their fault. They are ready to argue to defend themselves, but they don't learn anything, so they are repeaters. They are their own worst enemy, but you can't tell them this, it is too dangerous.

THREE-STEP CORRECTION PROCESS

To learn the proper lesson when you make a mistake, you must go through what I call the three-step error correction process.

Step one is admitting to yourself that you made a mistake. Even if you don't and someone else tells you, then you must accept the fact that it was your blunder and don't try to make excuses or involve others, or, worse, get angry and attack the one who tells you about your error. Anyone like this stops at level one of the error-correction process, and will be a repeater. They never learn.

Step two is a bit more difficult. You have to admit to others that the mistake was yours. Don't hide it or suppress the information because no one can help you if you won't talk about it. I know, many are more than willing to discuss your mistakes with you, but they make more mistakes than you do, and they are hung up at level one when you try to discuss their mistakes. Never mind that, concentrate on learning why you made the mistake and listen to anyone who wants to discuss it with you. You are now gathering all the information that you can about your error. Others may and can give you information that you never knew about. Don't shut off this very valuable source of information. Most people whom I know (especially your bosses) are more than willing to help and advise you when you come to them and say, "I made a mistake, can I talk with you about it and get some advice?" Most parents of teenage children would bless the day their children came to them with a question like that. The problem is 75 percent solved at this stage. A mistake has occurred, the individual admits it, and is open to discussion to learn from it. However, even if you can force yourself to go to level one or two of the error-correction process, it is not enough unless you go to the final or third stage.

The third stage is, what do you do about it? You admitted you were wrong. You discussed it with others, who agreed with you that it was your mistake and you now know all about the mistake, why it happened, the damage it caused, and, possibly, how to prevent it from happening again. Great! But, what are you going to do about it? The mistake may have been an error in judgment or a physical action in which some damage was done. You must now take corrective action that forces you to do something to correct the mistake or somehow compensate for the error, especially so if this corrective action is painful for you. You will remember how difficult it was for you to correct your mistake. It is this price or painful memory of the corrective action that will remain with you, and this is what stops you from being a repeater. You never want to have to go through that painful episode again, so you burn it in your memory forever. You won't repeat that mistake.

For example, at a party you spill a dish of food in the lap of a woman who is in a beautiful new gown. You ruined her dress. Do you apologize (step one), talk about it with others (step 2) and tell them how embarrassed you were, and let it go with that? Do you now proceed into level three, the correction level, and buy the woman a new gown to replace the one you ruined? Most won't go that far. You are truly sorry, but she is out $250 and you tell her you are sorry. Is that enough? You made a mistake and because you did not mean it, she pays the price. No! You pay the price if anyone must, and if you do, you will find you won't ever again spill a tray of food on anyone. You will be very careful.

At work you make a mistake that causes your company to lose a contract. You admit it, your boss says OK we all make mistakes. Now is that all or do you never rest until you personally get a new contract to replace the one lost due to your error? If you are like this, you are on the fast track, because all know you take corrective action when you make mistakes. If you use a process that goes beyond just words, then you can learn from

LEARNING FROM MISTAKES

your mistakes and always make new ones, never the same mistakes two or more times. In the navy, there is an old saying: "Every dog get two bites." If the dog makes the same mistake twice, then it is judged to be a repeater which is not able to learn from the mistake it made. The navy says two of the same kind are enough. Seems reasonable to me. What do you think?

POOR JUDGMENT: A FATAL FLAW

Sometimes people make mistakes due to incredibly poor judgment. You cannot teach anyone to have good judgment. They get it in childhood. When you meet them as adults and work with or for them, you see manifestations of good or poor judgment. It has little to do with formal education. It is an entirely different matter. It goes by the name of common sense or horse sense, but whatever you call it, those without it are repeaters. If you have poor judgment, you have my deepest sympathy, because neither this book nor any book, advice, or help you receive does you any good because poor judgment cancels it all out. You will be a repeater.

At work, if you are associated with employees who have demonstrated to you that they have poor judgment, run, do not walk, to the nearest exit, especially so if this person is your boss. They are walking time bombs, ticking away, waiting to explode. You won't go far professionally working with or for anyone with poor judgment. Your heart goes out to them in compassion, because they always seem to do the wrong thing at the wrong time or something happens to them over and over again. During my career, to date, I spent the better part of 15 years trying to help a person with poor judgment. He was always in some sort of scrape. Each and every time, it could easily be shown that he initiated the problem or compounded it by poor judgment. He is personally a very nice fellow, but he has caused a series of minor and a few major problems over and over again.

One time our secretary's watch stopped working. Joe (not his real name) asked her to let him look at it. He took the watch apart and brought it back to her, in pieces in an envelope. He said he could not fix it. I asked him if he knew anything about watches. He said, "No." Then why did he open it up in the first place? He said he thought he might "see something" inside and fix it. He apologized, but the secretary had to buy a new watch. Joe is likeable and tries to help, but who needs help like this? Such people are dangerous to your career. Help if you feel you must, but don't be around if Joe or those like him cause a major explosion. In such cases, it is only a question of time.

Everything in this book up to this point has been about mistakes. How depressing! Permit me to proceed into some more positive areas, and a very important one for the small business is serendipity.

SERENDIPITY

Serendipity is an "out-of-state" word for dumb luck. You set out to dig for coal and you find gold. You fall in love and get married; a few years later a distant relative of your spouse dies three thousand miles away, and your spouse inherits a small fortune. This is a case of serendipity, pure and simple, and it does not always happen to someone else. It happens all around you, but you must be aware it has just happened. Are you ready to react to take advantage of it?

One of our employees (let's call him George) told me one day that, at the computing center where we were working on a large government contract, an Air Force captain was watching the big automatic plotter print out the data that George was computing for another government client. The Air Force officer told George what a great program it must be to plot out such neat and precise plots. The officer went on to tell George how the officer's group was unable to learn how to write software to use the plotter properly, and their work was backing up. Here was an opportunity for new business for our company. Serendipity was talking to George, only he did not know it. I asked George if he knew who this officer was. He said he did not ask. I found out and sent our people to see him and we got a small contract to write programs to plot this data for his group. It also led to other new work as well. George told his associates that

LEARNING FROM MISTAKES

he was embarrassed, and he had better be careful what he said to me in the future, because he figured I must think he was dumb. George outdid me though. Serendipity struck again for George. His maiden aunt died and left him a big apartment building and other assets in the six-figure category. George resigned. I am still here. Napoleon was right when he said, "It is better to be lucky than good."

KEEP YOUR EYES OPEN FOR SERENDIPITY

You will go looking for new business and spend time, money, and great effort to win the contract. You got what you were after. Great! However, serendipity is always out there, and, when it approaches you, be ready to welcome it with open arms and change your game plan to suit it. Don't ignore it, as George did, because you are not listening when it knocks on your door. George got a second shot of serendipity, but you may not, so be ready.

Another major account came via two people walking into our office one day on the recommendation of a former associate. They offered us what proved to be a major and perennial contract. I did not know these people from Adam, but in they walked, with the opportunity any business person would give his eyeteeth to get. Again, we had to suddenly react, switch gears, redirect and reassign our people into the new target of opportunity, because, many times, an unplanned opportunity proves to be far more lucrative and rewarding than your original carefully thought out business plan. Don't be rigid and work with the blinders on. Look around, serendipity might be giving you the eye; you are not looking its way, so it looks at someone else and you never know that it went by.

A man owned a fish market, and he got requests for trash fish for his clients' cats. He found he was selling more trash fish than fish for people. He went into the cat food business, and now is one of the biggest in the market. A cigar manufacturer discovered he could earn more profit by investing his after-tax income from his cigar business in Certificates of Deposit and other financial investments than he could from expanding his cigar business. He now has his cigar business plus a far more profitable financial and investment company as well. Why not? They both recognized new business opportunities when they came their way.

IT'S LIKE LOVE: IT JUST HAPPENS, THAT'S ALL!

You can't create serendipity because it comes when it comes, but you can create and develop a hospitable climate in your organization so that when serendipity comes by, you are prepared to receive it and react to whatever it presents to you. Most times serendipity comes with a risk and you have to quickly decide if the risk is worth the potential reward; but you first have to recognize that a new and unexpected opportunity is at your office door, or even talking to you as it was in George's case. He did not recognize it, many do not. Some call it "luck," but even though luck exists, I believe it is random. If you really believe in luck, you have to conclude that some force is up there behind the scenes directing and tilting all of this good fortune toward someone and away from everyone else. Do you believe that? If you do, then go home, sit down, and wait for the knock on the door or for the telephone to ring. I hope you live long enough to receive the call or the visit.

CHANCE PLUS PREPARATION EQUALS LUCK

There is an old business saying, "The harder I work, the luckier I become." In football, it is called the Notre Dame bounce. The football seems to bounce more in Notre Dame's favor than in their opponents'. In baseball, "Yankee Luck" has been giving us Red Sox fans fits for years. When will it end? They come into Boston every September, and, year after year, they send us home in tears. Is God really a Yankee fan? Oh, I hope not! Give them an inch and they take the whole series. Give our guys an inch, and they give you back a yard, just to be polite. But I digress, back to business!

LEARNING FROM MISTAKES

The chances are high that you will run into serendipity in your small business. If you think about it, how many times in the past has serendipity run straight into you? What did you do? Did you welcome it or turn it away? If you can never recall in your life that serendipity touched you, then you just don't recognize it when it is near. If you are like that, then in your new business venture, you will, in all probability, never see it when it arrives. All is not lost if you feel this way. Go and hire some "lucky" man or woman who has shown, from past experience, that he or she and serendipity are on very familiar terms and let this person advise you when luck has arrived. It is far better though if you can recognize it, and then decide what to do about it. A mathematician friend of mine said that luck is the intersection of two lines, chance and preparation. When these two lines meet, here is your opportunity! Are you ready or do you keep on going, as if nothing had happened?

GOOD AND BAD THINGS WILL HAPPEN: ARE YOU PREPARED?

In summary then, wherever you work and whatever you do, you will make mistakes and you will also run into serendipity. How do you handle your mistakes? Do you learn from them and make them only once or are you a repeater? If you are not sure, ask your spouse. He or she knows, and will be only too happy to "help you see the light." Mistakes are a part of life. You should not be ashamed of them unless you just keep on making them over and over again.

Are you ready to recognize and react to the unexpected opportunity that may come with a risk attached? Change always involves risk. It entails going from the known to the unknown. Change is not good or bad, per se. Those of us who fear change in itself seldom "get lucky." Do you want a nice secure job that pays $25,000 per year come hell or high water, or do you want an opportunity, in which your income may fluctuate depending on the risks you take? Most, I think opt out for security too early on in life, and shut off all chances for serendipity to visit.

...K OFF: GO FOR IT!

...old saying, "There is no infallible way to win at ...there is an infallible way to never lose, and that is, ...chess."

Everyone has at least one good idea during his or her lifetime, and most of us have, at one time or another, thought about what it would be like to start up our own small business. Most do nothing about it, and many who try do not succeed, but it is better to have tried and failed than never to have tried at all, isn't it? Give it a go! Who knows where you may end up? You are just as good as everyone else you know. What have you got to lose? What have you to gain? Only you can decide, and only you can live with your decisions and choices, good, bad, or in between. If you have good basic judgment, you will know what to do when the time comes as your big chance approaches you. Everyone gets at least one and you can get more too, if you want to look for them. The more risks you take, the more mistakes you will make. Please remember the old saying, "The person who makes no mistakes, generally makes nothing." You only have to succeed once and the number of times you have failed does not matter then. We all can and do fail many times, but no one is a failure until he or she stops trying. Once you start, don't stop yourself, let someone else try to do that.

11

PERSISTENCE AND GOOD JUDGMENT: THE WINNING COMBINATION

PERSISTENCE IS MORALLY neutral. It is not good or bad per se. The conditions or circumstances under which you apply persistence make it good or bad. It is also known by other names; i.e., integrity, having the courage of your convictions, steadfastness, and consistency. These are the synonyms for persistence when others agree with you. When people don't agree with you, then the synonyms are stubborn, hard headed, fixed, rigid, unresponsive, and other words we cannot put down. The repeaters previously mentioned, who keep making the same mistakes, are persistent, but in a way are stubborn, hard headed, unchanging, and rigid. So, in these cases, it is not good to be persistent. However, persistence is a very desirable personal characteristic to possess, but only if it is accompanied by another very desirable personal characteristic, and that is good judgment. When should you be persistent and when should you yield, adapt, accept it, live with it, ignore it, or whatever? This calls for your good judgment.

PERSISTENCE AND POOR JUDGMENT EQUALS DISASTER

Unhappily, some of us have persistence and poor judgment, and that is a very bad combination. Hammering your head against a stone wall will just give you a broken head, but it is persistence, isn't it? Your headache will be persistent, too. I believe that most people do seem to have pretty good judgment, and most of the things they think about and say make a lot of sense. They are right more than they are wrong in their day-to-day judgments. Now if one could add a little persistence to go along with these ideas and good judgments and do something about them, we would be getting somewhere. Some persistence is called for and here is where many back off, let it go, and don't press it. It is too much trouble. People will argue with me and avoid me. I don't like being alone with everyone else on the other side. So you let some excellent new idea or plan go begging just because no one jumped up and welcomed you with open arms the first time you mentioned it. Would you keep writing books if your first 350 books or articles were all rejected? A very famous and successful author did just that before his first book was published. Boy, that is persistence, isn't it?

PERSISTENCE IS A SINE QUA NON IN BUSINESS

For anyone who wants to give it a go and start a small business, I can tell you, based on my own personal experiences, that, if you are not persistent and you have not been that way for all of your life, you are going to have a very rough time to survive. The odds against any new outfit surviving two or three years are bad enough anyway, but if, in addition to the cold, cruel statistics, you add the fact that the founder is not persistent, then his or her chances of failure are increased substantially.

In the 1950s, I was a bachelor living in an apartment building in Washington, DC. I used to like to sleep late on Saturdays, but that was a very busy day for salespeople who went through the apartment complex to sell their wares when the people were home from work. Salespeople would knock on my door starting around 8:00 A.M. and keep waking me up. So, I printed a "no salespeople" sign on a piece of paper and stuck it on the door, so I would be left undisturbed. It worked, except one Saturday a salesman woke me up. I asked him if he had seen the sign on my door. He said he had, but it was a torn, worn-out piece of paper and did not look good, so he sold me a nice plastic sign for a few dollars, with the words "No Salesmen" neatly printed on it. That is business persistence. Are you like that fellow or would you quietly pass by when you saw my sign on the door?

Another man I read about bought a large number of toilet seats via long distance, sight unseen, at a very low price, because it was a salvage from a train wreck. When several thousand seats arrived, he discovered they were for trailers and too small for houses. He could not return the merchandise as it was COD, so he stored them in his warehouse, but he kept thinking about them. He persisted and finally got an idea. He went to photography shops and sold the whole lot as novelty picture frames. They sold quickly and at a higher price than he had planned to sell them for originally. Would you have thought of something like that? These are examples of the sort of persistence and adaptability I am talking about for the small business person. Have you ever thought of or done something like that in your life before? If you can recall such situations and others called it clever or unusual, but you just knew what to do, then you may be the one to do it now in your new small venture as well.

A local university has a Small Business Advisory Council with a government grant to try to aid and assist those who are interested in starting up new ventures. I am a volunteer on the committee. I attended a meeting and the director of this council said that people come in every day with excellent ideas or products to produce, but when they are advised about the things they must do in order to get started, most leave and never return. The director gave the opinion that they were not persistent in trying to follow through even up to the point where they could begin looking for start-up capital, and that is when you really need persistence to be sure.

The director went on to say many wanted someone else to do these things for them. Ideas are great, and we all have some, but the trick is to make it happen. You need brains to have the ideas, but you need persistence to make it become a reality. Most will tell you that persistence is by far the most important single characteristic for making the small business go. If you tend toward laziness or relaxing and taking it easy, you will miss too many business opportunities, because persistence is a sine qua non to survive in the small business. Don't stop yourself, ever. Let someone else do that. Your competitors are out there every day looking for new business opportunities, and if you are not, they may grow at your expense, and rightly so if their persistence convinced one of your clients or customers to do business with them instead of you. That is the way our system works. The freedom to win is also the freedom to lose, and many times the difference is just persistence and little else. They keep going, and you do not. He/she wins and you lose. It follows, as Shakespeare says, "as the night follows day." Nothing good ever comes easy, we all know that.

THERE'S NO FREE LUNCH

You pay a price for whatever it is you want to gain. It takes a great deal of time and effort to make a business survive and grow. It is well for you to consider this fact before you start over. You cannot do it with a "lick and a promise"; other interests and demands upon your time and energies will conflict with your small business interests. I am not advocating that you shut off everything else and persist only in your business interests, no indeed. Those who do this end up with the business owning them, rather than the other way around. Once again, it is a question of judgment, however you had better prepare yourself for 60 to 80 hour weeks on a regular basis for at least a year or two during the start-up period. One of our associates was a brilliant and a very important and desirable part of the start-up team, but, "come hell or high water," when the clock struck 5:00 P.M., home he went. He would absolutely refuse to come in after hours and I don't think I ever saw him work on a Saturday. He was willing to go just so far in his commitment to making the company grow. Other less talented but more perseverant employees passed him up the ladder on the corporate structure. He even ended up working for one of his former subordinates, who passed him by. He told him the reason and he accepts it. He just will not work more than 40 hours a week, and most of the time we are lucky to get 40 hours of work from him, in any week. With his superior talent and ability, if he pushed a bit and gave some extra effort, I don't know what other things he could accomplish for himself and the company as well. He just is not persistent enough, at least, we don't think so.

Psychologists advise us that some of us enter what they call a "comfort zone," in which salary, lifestyle, and home life are comfortable and acceptable. When we enter this zone, we may lose ambition, drive, and persistence to continue pushing ahead at work to further improve our income, promotional opportunities, or further advancement. They just do not want to continue the effort when the worst or hardest part is behind them, and continued effort for a few more years could well pay off with exponential growth in their income. This "comfort zone" explanation fits the situation described above, and no one can alter it. It is an individual decision; further salary inducements or perks have no effect upon anyone who is fully satisfied with what he has at the moment.

KEEP GOING: NEVER STOP YOURSELF

Psychologists report that they were amazed to discover just how low a level this "comfort zone" is for so many people. Young people, in their early years, start out at a low salary, and work and persist to get raises and promotions to improve their position and income. Ambition and persistence run high. In about eight to ten years, the salary is sufficiently high that they start to coast. Continued or even more persistence, at this point, could well drive them to nearly the top of their chosen career in another five to ten years. But, the attraction of the "comfort zone" versus more hard work lures them away too soon and they never advance their real potential.

PLAY NOW—PAY LATER

This theory also applies to the Ph.D. discussed earlier in this book, who spent time during the working week enjoying his boat and left his 18 employees to work with minimal direction from him. He had it made until a few years later the recession of the early 1970s cut him down and ended it for him. Nothing that I know about is permanent, except death and taxes, neither of which are particularly attractive to me, but they are there. Everything else is subject to change and change can be for the better or worse. Your persistence in applying your energies in the areas you want to change can be very effective in producing change.

In business, you have your business plan, and you persist until it is achieved, and then you make another one and away you go again, until you reach your ultimate goal, whatever that may be (see Chapter 12). However, resting or turning your interests to other areas too soon only makes it more difficult to reach your goals. Why should anyone else push you toward your goals if you did not persist? Would you do that for anyone else? If so, why? Surely, you help anyone you can, but not, I trust, at the expense of your own career or business advancement. If you do, your reward may well come in the next world, but not in this one, I fear.

No business that I know of ever stays constant. It either goes up or down. It won't go sideways or remain level for very long. Factors within your organization and certainly macroeconomic factors are in a constant state of flux and they will affect your enterprise for good or ill. You have to be aware of what they are and persistent in your efforts to keep your outfit going upward for as long as you are able. If you become self-satisfied, smug, complacent, or rest in your "comfort zone," stand by for trouble.

I recently switched from one small supplier to another, after a number of years doing business with them, because the owner became unresponsive to our calls for service. One day at 10:30 A. M., he refused to service us because it was on a Wednesday and he said he does not work on Wednesday afternoons any longer. He closes his shop and takes a mid-week rest. He was afraid if he came over at 11:00 A. M., the job might extend beyond noon. Remember, I was talking with the owner, not the employees. Next, we called his office on a working day at 3:00 P. M. and no one answered the telephone. We called the next day and I asked him if something was wrong with his telephone, because no one answered our call of the previous day. He said his telephone was fine. He had gone to visit his mother the previous day for lunch and some relatives dropped by, whom he had not seen for years, so he did not go back and open his shop that afternoon. He had a very pleasant afternoon with his relatives, but he lost us as an account.

We called another outfit that is always prompt when we call for service or order supplies. Obviously this fellow was well into his "comfort zone." He did not even feel his telling me why he was not open would in any way affect our business relationship and I am sure our choosing another supplier does not bother him at all. He is still in business, but I wonder for how much longer? If he survives, my ideas and theories about small business are all wrong. Time will tell.

I can understand and appreciate why anyone would get discouraged and "throw in the towel" when they meet rejection and defeat. In spite of some heavy effort and persistence, they seem to be getting nowhere. However, why stop trying when you are succeeding? "Comfort zone" or not, I am amazed when I see some who are well on their way just slow down, lose interest, and grind to a halt when they are actually winning the game. I also can understand why changes in our personal lives—i.e.; divorce, illness, age, death of relatives, and problems with children—can affect how we view our business activities and change our priorities and interests. I have seen excellent and highly motivated people go into the doldrums after a divorce or after serious problems with their children. But, in most cases, after a few months, they accept the situation, adjust, put their life back in order, and return to their former level of interest, ability, and persistence. On rare and unfortunate occasions, they don't bounce back and it makes the bad situation worse. They deserve your help and understanding, if you can provide it, but it only works if they want to try again. If they don't they need assistance from medical and psychological personnel; you are not qualified to handle these situations, are you? Misdirected effort and persistence on your part in these unhappy situations are harmful to the individual, to your company, and to you, personally, as well.

PERSISTENCE AND GOOD JUDGMENT

I am a persistent person. I have always been so and I probably always will be so. I have made more than my share of misguided and misdirected efforts in trying to help individuals with unrepairable personality defects, or problems that I was unable to help them solve. It made matters worse. In the small company, close personal relationships can develop in which you want to help. Be careful here. You may do more harm than good. Persistence has its place, but know your limitations, and know why you are being persistent. Just being persistent in everything you do is being hard headed or just plain stubborn.

The areas in which persistence pays off are in sales and direction. You must have sales or you have nothing to do. Sales and new business will not take care of themselves and that is where you come in. Persistence here is for a specific, well-defined goal and it does pay off. Statistics from any sales department always tell the same story. Eighty to 90 percent of sales are made by 15 to 20 percent of the sales force. Why? The answer is persistence, pure and simple. In your small business, you may be chief executive, but you also are the chief salesperson. If not, you had better be. You'd better be quite a large company before you delegate this top, number-one priority to anyone else. More than one small outfit went under because the sales manager did not get enough sales to keep the small venture afloat.

FOLLOW THROUGH

The next most important area in which persistence pays off is in the area of direction within your small outfit. You give orders and instructions and leave the "how it's done" to your employees. You tell them what to do and when to do it, but they do it. Naturally you allow them to use their own talents and abilities to do the job. Don't oversupervise. That will stop you from growing; however do not undersupervise either. This leads to cost overruns, late deliveries, and other problems. When a delivery is due, make sure it is done. Be very insistent that costs are always within budget and each weekly milestone is achieved. If you are on a job with a 12-month delivery schedule and you lose just 4 hours a week, it does not seem too harmful week by week, but that is a 10 percent overrun. In a year, you are six weeks late and 10 percent overbudget for the entire effort.

Constant daily and weekly attention to these things prevent them from happening. Saturdays are for occasional use to get back on schedule and to meet next week's milestone. It is very easy to pick up an 8- or 12-hour slippage in a week's time, but you can't pick up six weeks' slippage during the last month of the job. Many try with double time and too much management interference at the end. It never works, but it does increase costs and add confusion at the worst possible time. We call it "seesaw management," too much direction at the start, too little in the middle, and too much at the end. Persistence and a constant level of direction keeps your "seesaw" from going up and down too much. This is not by any means a problem just for small outfits. I have seen it happen many times in big outfits; it has been my unfortunate experience to be personally involved in such affairs twice, and that was more than enough for me. Big outfits can go up and down on the seesaw and survive. They have staying power. The small outfit though may go up and down just once, and it is all over for them. An overrun on your first big job may put you out of business.

The reason why persistence is discussed in depth here is to emphasize that it is very important for the survival and growth of a small venture. If you are not a persistent person, nothing that I or anyone else writes or says to you will ever change you. We all are the way we are, and we can't change the way we think or our basic attitudes. We can suppress them or pretend for a while, but the toll on the individual is just too much to bear. You can't keep that up for very long. Forcing shy people to speak in public is cruel to watch. They just can't do it, and it upsets them too much to even try. It even upsets the audience.

If individuals, who are not persistent by nature, take on a major role in any new venture, they will have a very difficult time, because they just won't persist or push when the situation calls for it. The automatic "knee-jerk" response for anyone who is working in a small business should be persistence or even impatience, even to the point that someone has to tell you to back off a bit now and then. General George Patton said that most people have to be led, some driven ahead, but very few have to be restrained. In small business, if you are responsible, it is probably better for your company if you are one of those who must be restrained now and then. Persistence and impatience create activity and some action (results) as well. If it is not in you to be this way, you have an extra burden to carry with you in your small venture. If you are in a joint venture with co-owners, then one of you had better be very persistent and impatient, or else you may find, while you are all calmly, quietly, and patiently waiting for "it" to come to you, it all ends quietly before "it" arrives. You have to go out and get "it." If "it" arrives unexpectedly, are you persistent and quick enough to recognize it and respond to and capitalize upon whatever "it" is?

REMEMBER YOUR GOAL

There is a price that you pay when you are persistent and impatient in that you may carry this attitude home as well. You can't act one way from 8:00 A. M. to 5:00 P.M., and then become a completely different person when you go home. Your behavior tends to carry over outside of work, and there is a hazard to watch out for. You are doing all this at work for your family too, I assume. So, don't go overboard and forget about why you are doing all this work. If you are on an ego trip and the success of your venture is absolute and sole top priority in your life and you gain your goal, what do you end up with? You are wealthy and divorced with no friends. Of course that is better than being poor and divorced with no friends, but why not have them all? We pass this way but once. Some judgment in when to be persistent and impatient and when to hold off and make allowances for others, their attitudes, priorities, and goals and when you should compromise should be used. Your loved ones are at home, so try to leave the persistence, impatience, and perfectionism in the office where it belongs, and don't take it home where it does not belong. This little "trick," if you can ever do it, takes a great deal of practice, but it is well worth the effort to acquire this "dual personality" if you can. A hard driving, persistent, impatient but fair business executive is an excellent asset for any business, especially the small business, but at home a compassionate, understanding, and forgiving spouse and parent is far preferable. They are two different worlds for two different purposes. Try not to mix them. Each has its place and priority in your life. It is for you to choose what comes first, when push comes to shove, in the real world.

AGGRESSIVE BUT NEVER OFFENSIVE

You can be persistent and impatient without being offensive. It depends upon your personal style. You can be aggressive without being offensive. Again, it depends upon your style. The main difference between the "hard" versus the "soft" sell is the persistence of the salesperson. Being attentive and constant with your client is a form of persistence. Records and my own experience have taught me that the "hard" sell is far superior to the "soft" sell in making the sales you are after.

The same is true in directing your operation. If you are too understanding or too embarrassed to correct mistakes and administer fair discipline when it is due, then stand by for a repeat performance. If you are persistent and insist that your instructions and directives are carried out and you carefully monitor your operation to make sure that they are, you will get what you want. W. Somerset Maugham said, "It's funny, if you insist on only the best, then that's what you will get."

My wife's cousin was an accountant for a small company with two partners. One was a no-nonsense, persistent, hard-driving businessman and the other was Mr. Nice Guy. She told us she would hear the two owners argue openly in the office over many things, especially about the directing of the employees. Mr. Nice told Mr. Persistent he was being far too hard on his people by making them get to work on time, allowing no early departures, and strictly adhering to schedules. They argued so much they finally split up the company and my wife's cousin was offered a job with both outfits. She chose Mr. Nice, and nine months later, Mr. Nice was bankrupt. So she got a job with Mr. Persistent's rapidly growing new outfit. There is a lesson there I think, don't you? I wouldn't go as far as Leo Durocher, in what he says about nice guys, but Mr. Durocher isn't too far off the mark either. If you don't know what he said, ask a baseball fan. He or she will know.

DISCIPLINE

Discipline is a subset of persistence. Self-discipline comes first. If you cannot discipline yourself, you will find it very difficult to apply discipline to anyone else. Unfortunately, discipline is a necessary part of life in the business world. You may think that founders of small businesses, or co-owners, would automatically work harder and show much more interest in advancing the new company's fortunes than they would as employees in some big outfit in which they would never share in or benefit from corporate growth or profit. This is just not true. I have seen, read, and heard about many situations in which the exact opposite occurs. Here is the "reasoning" if you want to call it that. For years, these people were always being supervised by someone else, with rules, company policies, and procedures to follow. Discipline, order, and precedence were the rules. Now they are bosses of their own little ventures. No rules, no policies from above, and complete freedom to do it all, when, where, and how they please. How marvelous for them. Now what do some of them do? For the first time in their lives, they are free to do whatever they want at work. They find they have little or no self-discipline. No one tells them to finish the proposal by 10:00 A.M. next Friday. No one complains to them if they don't get the follow-on contract. No one tells them to reduce or control costs because profits are dropping. No one makes them do anything, so they let "little" things slide or "little" problems go uncorrected.

Work starts at 8:00 A.M. and the owner floats in around 8:30 A.M. or so. He or she also leaves early whenever he or she likes. I don't have to draw you a road map. You know what the employees will do, don't you? It is the old kid's game of follow the leader. They will drift in and out just as the boss does. They really like the friendly informality of the boss's operation. It is far superior to their former place of employment where they would be severely disciplined or even lose pay if they arrived late. You can also predict what eventually happens to such a small venture—another name on the corporate casualty list.

SELF-DISCIPLINE IS ACQUIRED

So, if you do not have self-discipline, you may have persistence, but you won't always apply it properly or consistently. Persistence is like your IQ. You are born with it, and as you grow, you become increasingly aware of your abilities. However, that is only your potential. You have to work at it in order to turn this potential talent into some actual results. The self-discipline is turning your potential energy into kinetic energy to get something done. I don't think you can become persistent if it is not part of your individual makeup, however self-discipline is an acquired (not inherited) characteristic. You can become self-disciplined if you want to be so. It takes a great deal of your effort if you don't like it, but it can be done. You can lose 30 pounds if you want to. You just have to decide to do it, and pay the price while you shed the excess weight. Self-discipline is a sine qua non for the small business person. Let's leave it at that.

Now let's assume you have self-discipline. You are first in and last out. Great! Now can you discipline others? The old canard of money-grubbing business persons who manipulate and abuse their employees is just that, a canard. The vast majority of big or small business managers whom I know are all very concerned about the welfare and careers of their people. Many of these business people spend a great deal of their time and effort in doing all they can for their employees. That is all well and good, and it is well worth it because it is the right thing to do. It fosters loyalty and high morale when the employees know the boss won't ever do anything to hurt them for his or her own personal or immediate gain. I have seen a small business owner turn down an offer to buy his outfit; he would have been set for life, then and there. He told me that the main reason he rejected the offer was his fear of what would happen to his faithful employees if they were swallowed up in a strange new big outfit. He feared they would lose their jobs, because the buyer was after his clients and did not need his staff all that much. This is admirable and more people than you might think feel this way about their staff. The boss is the parent figure and everyone knows everybody else on a first name basis.

DISCIPLINE MUST BE TIMELY

However, this makes it rather difficult to apply discipline when needed for the good of the company. Most managers find it difficult to apply discipline to others even when they are self-disciplined themselves. When I met my first serious attitude and behavior problem, it was as a middle manager in a large electronics company. This employee was really something. He got me into problem after problem, and my boss wanted me to fire him. I begged off, told my boss the fellow had a wife and three children, and what would they all do if I fired the provider? My boss said you do it now or you will end up in six months with far bigger difficulties. I still did not have the courage to do it.

One Saturday morning, I was at home taking a bath. The doorbell rang and my wife answered it. It was my problem guy, let's call him Joe (not his real name). Joe asked to see me and my wife told him I was upstairs taking a bath. Joe rushed by my wife, up the stairs, and entered the bathroom, with his wild eyes sticking out too far. He said he had to see me about his problems at work. I told him as Churchill did when a similar situation happened to him, that he could see I had nothing to hide. Anyway, I had to tell him to get out while I dried off and got dressed. I won't go into his "reasons" for having to see me then and there. You would not believe me anyway. Incredibly, I still did not fire him. Sure enough, as my boss had said, Joe created a big problem at work, and I and my boss ended up in the general manager's office to explain. Fortunately the big boss had a sense of humor, and when I told him about our bathroom conference, he enjoyed that very much.

Joe was immediately dismissed and I got a gentle dressing down from the general manager and told never again to let such things go uncorrected. I never did it again. I can now discipline and dismiss anyone for cause, and it does not affect me personally any longer. Bathroom Joe, if he had been with me at the start of the small venture, would have severely damaged my company as well as me. I am glad I learned this lesson about discipline early in my management career. Most of us wait far too long before we get down to the discipline, especially if dismissal is called for, and it sometimes is.

A year back, we had an employee who just could not get to work on time. She lived within two miles of the office, yet each day she had another excuse for being late. She was warned verbally twice. At the second warning, I told her to get up 15 minutes earlier each day. Her reply startled me. She said, "I don't have to get up early, because I live so close to the office." With this response in mind, I felt it necessary to issue a formal, written warning that any more tardiness would lead to her dismissal. Several days later, she was late again. We dismissed her, got a new and better qualified replacement, who is always prompt, courteous, and responsive. The whole office staff felt much better. See how easy it is if you can face up to discipline when it is called for and justified?

The general informality of the small business can lead to a lack of formal office discipline. It is up to you to recognize the need and apply it when necessary. The tendency is to wait too long or try to correct it informally, and it does not usually work out too well. I have made all of the mistakes I am discussing, so there is no need at all for you to reinvent the wheel and make the same mistakes in your small business. You know when you have to do it, don't you? You don't want to? Well neither does anyone else. It is your job to do it. Well then, who will do it for you but you? Doctors cannot save all of their patients. Teachers cannot pass all of their students. That is part of life. If you get so upset that you cannot apply fair, honest, and just discipline when it is necessary, well you know who will pay the price, don't you?

In summary then, persistence is a requirement for the small businessperson, and self-discipline and the ability and courage to apply fair discipline to your employees are very important as well. Never act in anger. Go home, cool off, and if you still feel in the morning that discipline is required, then go in and do it. Firing or disciplining anyone in anger can result in lawsuits at worst, and decreased morale and fear from your other employees at best. You don't need either one at any time. It is very good if your people respect you, but not so good if they fear you at work. In many cases, the difference between respect and fear is the way you handle bad situations or disciplinary problems that will come up from time to time, whenever you work, whatever your position, and whatever you do.

12

HOW AND WHEN TO BAIL OUT

FEW THINGS are more difficult to handle than a guest who stays too long. The party is over and just about everyone has departed, except one or two who seem to be enjoying themselves so much that they overstay their welcome. You walk through the room, winding the clocks, or mention loudly to your spouse about your early morning appointment, but to no avail. When they finally take their leave, you smile politely, shut the door behind them, and promise yourself that you will never have another party, or if you do you won't invite Mr. and Mrs. "Stay Too Long" again. There is no permanent harm done, however, and in a few weeks, all is forgiven and forgotten.

GO WHILE THE GOING IS GOOD

In business though, the damage done by a founder staying on too long can be serious and even disastrous. Don't make the mistake of staying too long. Plan for your departure. Of all the mistakes you can make along the way, if you survive and grow and it looks like your outfit is on its way, you can make one final mistake that can cancel out years of successful effort up to that point. Staying too long can be costly. The first big mistake you can make, if you don't plan ahead for your departure, is to die in the saddle. Now that doesn't do you much good at all, does it? Your years of hard work and building your company to a nice going concern lead you to a nice funeral, flowers for the widow, and you personally don't benefit any further. In addi-

HOW AND WHEN TO BAIL OUT

tion, your demise can lead to the demise of your venture as well, if you remained the key person for too long, who made all of the important decisions and ran the show directly, day by day, and no one else was prepared to take over. You were on an ego trip and in today's parlance, "your ticket was cancelled" at a point where you did not want to get off.

Corporations are immortal, but people are not. Please remember this. With this in mind, it is a very good idea for you to plan for your own departure and give yourself plenty of time to groom your replacement, and when the time comes, go, in heaven's name, go.

DON'T IGNORE HISTORY OR YOU'LL REPEAT THE MISTAKES

Business history reveals time and time again that the founders of any new venture do not do as well financially as those who later take over the going concern and really expand the business. There are good reasons why this is so. The entrepreneur is a different breed of cat from the bureaucratic manager. In fact, most entrepreneurs or creative types do not like bureaucrats, lawyers, or CPAs. It is not exactly personal. Entrepreneurs want to wheel and deal and gamble, and do all sorts of new things. It is their nature. The lawyer, CPAs, bureaucrats, and cooler heads are always telling them, "You can't do that," or "Not now, the market isn't right," or "We have to do the paperwork first and that will take time."

They are probably right, but successful entrepreneurs can tell you many stories about the times in the past when they just ignored their accountants and lawyers and plunged ahead. The majority who do this fail, but some survive and grow, and they develop an attitude that what worked before will work again and again. This is not true, but try selling that to a president of a $20 million a year company who started alone with a few others, working in his cellar or garage. There were no lawyers or CPAs around then, so why does he or she need them now? Go ahead and try to tell the president that he or she should step down because the company has expanded beyond his or her abilities to manage it well. The job you lose will be your own.

In many cases, the founder is kicked out by stockholder pressure, the board of directors revolt, or some other unhappy situation. Do you want this to happen to you, at the point in your life and career when it is time to enjoy the fruits from years of your successful work? You probably can be well taken care of if you will only cooperate.

Plan ahead for a certain point in which you will voluntarily step down. You ran a good race. You brought the company from zero up to where it is today. Now it is someone else's turn to take the baton from your hands and proceed with the next phase of the endless relay race. (I hope your company wasn't a 100-yard dash.) You can go voluntarily or be forced out kicking and screaming and have it all end up in court (you will probably lose). I know, it is your baby and you breathed life into it; nothing would be there to argue about at all if it weren't for you. You can point backwards to the countless times you saved the day like the U.S. cavalry, rushing to the rescue, but that is in the past. We are talking about today and the future. You must let go.

Again, the analogy between the human and the corporate body holds true. You have a child and for 20 years or so you do everything for the child. He or she grows up. You want a scientist, but he wants to be a sheep herder in the big sky country. You want her to be a doctor and you get a go-go dancer. All you can do is hope that your handiwork will work out eventually, but you have to let go, accept it, and carry on. Something similar occurs in your corporate body. There is a time when you must turn it over to someone else and let go. If you plan it and work with your successor, you have an excellent chance that your corporate culture or the basic principles will continue along similar lines. If you don't and you are forceably removed, you may see your corporate baby end up in foreign hands and change dramatically into quite a different thing from what you intended or want it to be.

BUREAUCRATS INHERIT THE WORLD

A one-person show can only grow up to a limited size, then the bureaucrats must take over, or it won't continue growing. You are the bottleneck, and everyone is afraid to tell you. The best way to avoid it is to plan ahead to a point in which you will step down. It may be age, or a point where sales cross a set number, or some other objective and measurable number. As that point nears, you will start to find "reasons" why you should not leave. That is human. If you really are as important as you think you are, others will come to you, tell you so, and ask you to stay on. If no one brings it up, then look at yourself and remember the plan. The military has strict rules on when you go and it is age. In exceptional cases—i.e., MacArthur and Rickover—special arrangements are made but you really don't think you are one of these, do you? Remember, if you are, others will tell you this. If only you think so, well, you know what that means as well as I do.

DON'T HURT YOURSELF AT THE END

Staying on too long is a serious mistake. I would rate it up around a nine or ten on the scale. You can hurt yourself more than the company at this stage of the game. The company is middle size or so, has a nice backlog of work, probably the stock is selling well on the public market. It can survive without you. Great! Now it is time for you to divest yourself of some of your shares for a perfectly valid and acceptable business reason. You are retiring. You announce it six months or a year in advance, so no one is upset when you sell out a large percent of your shares over the six- to twelve-month period. Everyone understands this. It is time for you to go. You may stay on the board of directors with some nice perks and an annual income to thank you for your cooperation with your successors. They will gladly do this if you cooperate. If you don't and they have to push and shove you a little, then hard feelings arise and you are alone against the world. Few win such a battle.

DON'T LOOK BACK

Also, when you leave, please leave. Let them give you a big farewell party, and name the new laboratory after you, but don't keep coming back and making a pest of yourself. They want to treat you with courtesy and respect, but if you keep dropping by to tell old "war stories" and to "help out" the new boss, that just makes it difficult for all concerned. Go and enjoy life. Get up, say a few words of encouragement about how well your successors are doing and sit down. That can even help the price of your stock to rise even higher if you retained any. If you sold it all, then you have no business even being at the stockholder's meeting. It is not your baby any more, you sold it all, didn't you?

If, after you have gone, employees want your help or advice, they will call you. If they don't, don't call them just to see how things are going. They don't want to talk to you. They have a new boss now and it is not you. Please accept that, as hard as it is to sink in. Let them be as loyal and hardworking and devoted to the new boss as they were to you. If you interfere, one of two situations usually follows. If your former associates listen to you and do what you suggest, you create confusion for the new management and they will move in fast to stop it. The other situation is more likely to happen. Those whom you try to contact will shut you off either politely or rudely, and in either case, you will be hurt personally. So, don't do it. You can't benefit in either situation.

Don't be like the artist I read about. He went to a big art exhibit and saw one of his earlier drawings on display. He had sold it years ago. He looked it over and decided it needed a little touching up here and there, so he pulled out a drawing pencil and started to "fix it up a bit." He was arrested of course, and his claim that the work of art was his creation, so he had every right to work on it, fell on deaf ears. It did not belong to him any longer. He drew it and sold it, regardless of how he feels about his own work. Your corporate creation is no longer yours when you leave. It is the responsibility of someone else, regardless of how you feel about it.

HOW AND WHEN TO BAIL OUT

Again, the human analogy holds true. Most marital problems occur at the start of the marriage during the period of adjustment, and many divorces follow within two or three years of the happy event. After thirty years or so, the kids are grown up, empty-nest syndrome sets in, both partners retire, are home 24 hours a day and they drive each other up the wall. A number of separations or divorces flare up after many years together, and at a time when the few remaining years should be the best. No financial problems, time to enjoy life, and being grandparents, but no. Strife and struggle set in and wipe it all out.

The corporation has similar tendencies. Most fail to survive the first few crucial years, and the corporate equivalent of divorce follows, and that is bankruptcy. Years later, when the corporation is a growing and healthy adult, the older founders refuse to let go or to leave quietly and an upheaval follows at a time when they are older and looking forward to a well-earned and happy time of life after years of hard work, struggle, and some success in spite of the odds against it. What a terrible way to end it all! You can prevent it by, as said earlier, planning for your own departure in an orderly and predictable manner.

In all of the struggle and corporate strife I have read about concerning the departure of a recalcitrant owner, I have never once heard about the individual owner winning the battle. A close business associate always says, "Don't look back on a deal." When it is over, it is over. Please remember it is very likely that those who will take over from you will do far better financially than you did. It is the nature of business. It is very difficult to get it started and on the way, and much easier to expand a going concern. You might spend 10 to 20 years getting your company up to $5 to $10 million a year in sales. The new management gets it up to $50 million within five years after you leave. They knew how to do this and you did not, so accept it and forget it. It may satisfy your ego to watch it decline into bankruptcy after you leave, but that won't do your financial situation much good, will it? Your post-retirement perks will stop and the stock you kept becomes worthless. That is no way to gratify your ego about how important you were, is it?

WORRY ABOUT YOURSELF AT THIS STAGE

Don't worry about what anyone else gets or does not get. Why don't you cheer them on to even greater heights so your stock becomes even more valuable for you and your loved ones? In starting the new business, you chose a role very similar to army or marine assault troops. Their job is to go ashore first and face the fiercest fighting. Most of them get hit on the beach. Casualties are 50 to 80 percent before they go one mile inland and establish the beachhead. However, when they succeed, up comes the biggest part of the force to exploit the beachhead and rush inland with very low casualties. They win the final victory. Very few members of the assault troops ever get to march in the victory parade. They are not around any more, or if they are, they are in the hospitals unable to march and receive the honors given out to the victors. That's the way it is.

But, of course, you knew this when you started out, didn't you? If not, you learned it very quickly as you saw your fellow entrepreneurs falling all around you. You survived. Good for you! Now don't fight it at the end. Take what you earned, enjoy it, and don't look back on the deal and concern yourself with the fact that those who took over from you get a bigger piece of the victory banquet than you do. You chose the most dangerous role. Others chose a different role, to wait and take over from you later on. There is a place for each one, and even though I fully agree with those who feel it is not "fair" for the entrepreneurs to get the least if they succeed, that is the way it is. As President Kennedy said so well, "Life isn't fair, it just is the way it is," or to put it another way, when you raise your head in silent prayer and say "Why me?", if you listen carefully, you will hear an answer, "Why not?"

TIME IS RUNNING OUT

Mistakes made at the end have one other very important aspect that makes them even more serious and permanent. You are running out of time. Of all the things you can waste, time is the one precious thing that you cannot recover. You make a mistake and lose money (I have done that a lot), but you can recover it on the next job you do. You can make a mistake and argue with a friend, but you can later make up, or, if you must, find new friends. But time, once gone, is gone forever. One irreverent thinker said, "Even God can't change the past for if He did, He would have to contradict Himself." What's done is done! It is over, but lost time or a mistake made when you have not enough time to repair it is a bad mistake to make. (That is how I justify being impatient. Not bad, is it?)

Any mistake at any time and at any place can harm you or someone else, but, in most situations, if you learn from your mistakes, you can come out of it a better and wiser person. Most of us get smart slowly and get old quickly, but as we mature (people don't get old any more, they "mature"), our error or mistake rate should diminish as experience and hopefully wisdom replace youthful vim and vigor. So, don't end it all with a big, final mistake of staying on too long beyond your ability to perform well, if your company truly outgrows your ability to handle it well. Once again, it is your decision and your choice, but please don't do this one wrong. It is probably the last big business decision you will have to make, so do it right, leave on time, and good luck. If within a few months after your departure they come to you and ask you to return because they need and want you back, you can come back if you like, ego flying high, and save the day. If you believe this will happen, you also believe in the tooth fairy.

13

DELANEY'S BUSINESS LAWS AND GUIDELINES

WHEREVER YOU WORK and whatever you do, people are people. You can never really predict individual behavior, because sometimes an individual will suddenly switch on you and really surprise you. You can end up delighted or disappointed by a sudden and remarkable change in individual behavior or performance, however group behavior is something else again. People of certain types do seem to behave in a similar way most, if not all, of the time. So one can generalize with a certain degree of accuracy. Permit me to list some, what I call "Delaney's Business Laws and Guidelines" that I have noted over the years. I have quoted all the way from Napoleon to Yogi Berra, plus a few of my own.

I have read this list a few times to audiences at the end of my boring speeches on small business, and many later asked me if I had ever worked where they work, because they could put names in most of the items listed. See if they apply to you and where you work. If you come up with some I have overlooked, or some new ones, let us hear them.

1. The closer that people live to the office, the later they arrive each morning.
2. Those who arrive late also tend to leave early.
3. There is a strange virus that seems to make people fall "ill" the day before or after a holiday.
4. Show me any company's sick leave records and I will show you the paydays. Only people on the critical list are absent on payday.
5. Most bad rumors come true. Most good ones don't.

6. When you ask someone what time it is, and he or she does not know, he or she may give you a weather report.
7. If we know what to do, we do it. If we don't know what to do, we talk about it. If we don't know how to talk about it, we write a report about it.
8. No decision is the worst decision.
9. A camel is a horse put together by a committee.
10. The length of the answer to any question is in inverse proportion to the validity of the answer.
11. The boss is not always right, but the boss is always the boss.
12. God is on the side with the heavy artillery.
13. The worst thing about being dumb is you don't know you're dumb. The worst thing about being smart is you know you are smart. The former is difficult to work with and the latter impossible.
14. One percent of something is better than 100 percent of nothing.
15. Victory has a thousand fathers; defeat is an orphan.
16. Ten percent of any group does 90 percent of the work.
17. Ten percent of any group needs psychiatric attention.
18. There is absolutely no free lunch. Somebody pays.
19. You get help in proportion to the help you give, but not from the same people.
20. It's not over until it's over, and then it's not over.
21. Generally those who never make mistakes never make anything.
22. If, at work, you have to choose between being liked or respected, choose respect.
23. If you succeed, you will be called lucky. If you don't you will be called stupid.
24. You are a success when you say you are, and not before.
25. No one is indispensable, not even you.

14

RECOGNIZE MISTAKES AND BENEFIT FROM THEM

ANYONE WHO CHOOSES to start or operate a small venture knows or quickly learns that they are very fragile and easily injured. Macroeconomic forces, over which we have absolutely no control, affect the small business first and hardest. The general economic cycle may reduce sales and profit for the big companies for a while, however they will survive, but many small outfits cannot. We can't do much about this except to know it is there and keep an eye out for the signs that a downturn is coming and do the best we can. However, there are many things we can do that are our own decisions and choices that later lead to survival, growth, and success or to bankruptcy.

The corporate coroners, who review the "bodies," report management failure as the main reason. That is true, but that is like saying the main reason for divorce is marriage. What are these management mistakes? Are they deadly? Can you make some, learn, and recover and go on, or are some so deadly that once is too much? There are many kinds of illnesses that beset the human body. There are many kinds of mistakes that beset the corporate body. Some human illnesses are fatal in themselves and all that can be done is to put the patient at ease as much as possible, reduce the discomfort, and count the days or weeks. Some illnesses or injuries are minor in themselves, however the person involved refuses to recognize or treat the minor illness and lets it go unattended; these can build up into a major crises with fatal results. You can make fatal or very serious business mistakes that destroy your business immediately, and you just have to count the days, weeks, or months and watch it happen. You can make minor mistakes, ignore and repeat them, let them accumulate, and they can build up to fatal proportions. The only difference is it takes a bit longer to happen, that's all.

My father was a fireman, and, as a young boy, I well remember his stories around the dinner table. Most fires could have been prevented for very little expense. Most people who died in fires were not burned. The flames rarely reach them. Their deaths are due to other causes—smoke or panic—because they were unprepared to deal with the emergency situation. Their actions made matters worse because they did not know what to do. Likewise, many small businesses fail because the owners did not know the real reason that was causing the problem to occur, or if they did, they did not know what to do about it. This book is mostly concerned with "fire prevention." It is intended to alert the reader to some fairly typical situations that can, have, and will occur in the small business, and how to prevent them from happening to you. When the fire alarm goes off, it is too late for you to quickly read the instructions on how to operate the foam fire extinguisher hanging on the wall or to read the fire escape route map for your building. I still remember what my Dad told us a thousand times, so when I enter a restaurant, theater, or hotel, the first things I look for are the emergency exit signs. My spouse and kids call me the safety chief, but I still do it. It is part of my heritage. I hope I never have to run for the fire exits, but if it ever happens, I will know where to go. We also carry a flashlight in our suitcase when we stay at hotels. It is a good $3.00 investment, isn't it?

One day a delivery truck pulled up in front of our office to deliver some supplies. The driver jumped out as smoke started to emerge from under the hood. A small fire started. He did not know what to do. One of our guys saw him standing there doing nothing, so our guy took one of our fire extinguishers, ran out, and put out the fire before it reached the gas tank. The driver of the truck just stood there watching. Later I advised our guy he had risked his life; he should have given the extinguisher to the driver and let him do the honors. Our guy told me the driver was in panic and just stood there. If that truck had exploded, it would have involved our office as well as those inside, so I guess our guy did the right thing. The point I am making is be prepared; you never know when a mistake or an emergency will erupt right in front of you. Do you know what to do or do you stand there, frozen in panic, and let it all get worse?

EARLY AND LATE MISTAKES ARE THE WORST KINDS

Of the many mistakes one can make in business, those that are the most serious seem to happen right at the start or at or near the end. If you distribute stock to the wrong personnel, you can't change it. A mistake made right at the start will result in an automatic irreversible set of circumstances that builds like an avalanche. You cannot stop or reverse it later. Be very careful here. This mistake is forever. Next, if you merge and make a mistake, you cannot go back and "unmerge" later. One shot and that is it. Don't hurry any merger. Keep in mind you are selling your outfit once and for all. Sell in haste and repent at your leisure. Also, please remember the post-merger statistics. The seller's officers generally depart within 18 months of the sale, either voluntarily or they are put out. If you go public and sell off majority ownership, this is not completely irreversible, but you may have some difficulty trying to retain operational control, and you may lose it. Staying on too long at the end is another very serious mistake. Problems stemming from this mistake can severely injure you personally. Your company may well survive at this stage, but you may not do too well.

All of the in-between mistakes can be handled as long as you don't panic. In your fear or ignorance of what to do, you compound the problem by another mistake made in trying to correct the first one, or worse, you ignore the mistake, refuse to admit it is there, and you let it lie there, uncorrected, to fester and flare up later again and again. Please remember that running out of money is not the cause of any problem. It is the effect of some other problem that causes you to run out of cash. You may have no sales, or your costs are getting too high, or

RECOGNIZE AND BENEFIT FROM MISTAKES

your accounts receivable lie uncollected, or you are very busy but you don't seem to have any profit left over at the end of the month. Don't mistake the effect for the cause. If you do, you will spend your time trying to solve the wrong problem, and it will only repeat.

NOTHING MYSTERIOUS, JUST COMMON SENSE

Having read this far, you can see that there is nothing mysterious or esoteric in the preceding chapters. You already know about this material. It is common sense, so why belabor the obvious? Unfortunately, it is exactly for these reasons that most small businesses fail. They forgot about some obvious thing that causes damage later, and they never recover. Hope springs eternal and currently 600,000 new ventures are started each year, recession or not. At the same time, 10,000 outfits go bankrupt each week. These failed entrepreneurs started out a year or two ago with high hopes, all set to succeed. There is no magic formula or secret to survive and grow. It is just plain common business judgment and decisions by the persons who run the business. Years ago, we had to pay higher interest rates for our monthly working capital loans because of actions taken by French President DeGaulle. We were able to survive it, but if not, I hardly could blame the President of France if we had gone under; some did go under then due to sudden increased costs for business loans. Even if I did blame President DeGaulle, so what? If you get killed by accident or due to your own mistakes, does the reason really matter to you then? Hardly!

PLAN YOUR BUSINESS VENTURE

The intent of this book is to list a series of some very common causes of business failure, so you will avoid them as much as possible. In planning your new venture, you had better plan beyond just getting started. The young couple, deeply in love who happily plan for the marriage but do not plan any further, are in for a rude awakening when they return from the honeymoon and find that the marriage was only the beginning, not the end, of their plans. Now they have to make it work and unhappily many find out, to their later sorrow, that they were unable or unwilling to do so. So, plan your new venture beyond the start date. In the throes of enthusiasm, before you get started, you may make a mistake that later comes back to haunt you. When I look back to the days before we actually started and remember the things I wanted to do with our stock, I blush with embarrassment. My corporate Guardian Angel was sitting right on my shoulder, because I was unable to do all that I had planned. I know now if I had done what I wanted to do then, we would not have survived beyond one or two years, if that long. So, don't be dumb, as I was. Do it right the first time, and don't be afraid to give it a go, because, if someone like me can survive for so long, you can do it too. Good luck.

INDEX

A

Accelerated depreciation, 62
Accounting problems, 60–63
  cash versus accrual, 60–61
  depreciation methods, 62
  determining your fiscal year, 62
Accounting systems, cash versus accrual, 60–61
Accrual accounting system, 60–61
American Bar Association, 32
Annual reports, 145

B

Bankruptcies, statistics on, 5
Behavior at work and at home, 177–78
Blue-chip stocks, definition of, 141
Bureaucracy, 116–18, 149
Business cycles, 80–82
Business plans:
  capital and, 23–24
  elements of good, 22–23
  flexibility in, 16–17
  highly detailed, 20–21
  imitation of, 25–26
  importance of having, 14–15, 24–25
  mistakes made in, 14–28
  planning backward, 21–22
  revising, 17–18
  unrealistic, 18–20
Buy/sell agreements of stock, 41–42
Bylaws:
  how to develop, 32–33
  mistakes in, 42–43

C

Capital:
  how to obtain, 34–35
  lack of working, 71–72
  loans from banks, 10–11
  plans and, 23–24
  selling shares to get start-up, 34

Cash accounting system, 60–61
Cash reserves, 79–80
Clients:
  impressing, 106–8
  raising prices and, 110–11
  refusing jobs and, 109–10
  underpricing and, 110
  your prosperity and, 108–9
Columbus method of planning, 15
Corporation, 30
  bylaws formation and, 32–33
  legal advice and, 31–32
  shareholders and, 33
Cost accounting, 72–74

D

Debts, 76–77
Decision making and emotions, 95–97
Departure (from your company), 186–93
  benefits of your, 189
  bureaucrats and your, 189
  planning for your, 187–88
  staying too long, 186–87
  time and your, 192–93
Depreciation methods, straight line versus accelerated, 62
Diaper management, 149
Discipline:
  necessary, 64, 179–80
  self-, 100, 179, 180–81
  sexual harassment and, 97
  timing of, 181–82
Dun & Bradstreet, 76

E

Economic darwinism, 5, 81
Electronic News, 4, 80
Emotions and decision making, 95–97
Employees:
  familiarity and, 89
  favoritism and, 96

Employees (*cont.*)
  growth and new, 115–16
  lawsuits and, 97
  mergers and, 126, 128
  nepotism and, 44, 97–99
  progress reports and, 93–94
  salaries of, 116
  stock and, 36–38, 39
  See also Personnel
Expenses, going public and, 145–46

F

Favoritism, 96
Financial problems, 70–83
  bad debts, 76–77
  cost accounting, 72–74
  free spending, 77–80
  growth versus profit, 74–75
  ignoring business cycles and, 80–82
  undercapitalization, 70–72
Fiscal year, determining your own, 62

G

Going public, 140–53
  cost of, 145–46
  external factors affect the price of your stock, 150–51
  internal company changes after, 149–50
  mistakes in, 141
  preparation of a prospectus, 146–47
  selling personal shares after, 151–53
  selling shares too quickly, 141–42
  selling too many shares and, 143–45
  setting too low a price and, 142–43
  timing of, 143
  trading on insider information, 147–49
Growth:
  bureaucracy and, 116–18
  diminishing returns, 114–15
  impressing clients and, 106–8
  new employees and, 115–16
  new jobs and, 109–10
  persistence and, 176
  pricing of your product and, 110–12
  prosperity and, 108–9
  remedies for growth plans, 106–19
  versus profit, 74–75, 112–13
Gumpert, David, 3

H

Harvard Business Review, 3
Humphrey, Hubert, 8

I

Industry price-earnings ratio, 150

J

Judgment, poor:
  mistakes and, 161–62
  persistence and, 168–69

K

Kennedy, John Fitzgerald, 192
Kubik, J. Fred, 3

L

Laissez faire system, 6
Law of diminishing returns, 114–15
Lawsuits:
  employees and, 97
  prospectuses and, 146–47
Lawyers:
  by experience, 158
  forming a corporation and, 31–32
  from others, 157–58
  how to choose, 32
  preparation of a prospectus, 146
  poor judgment and, 161–62
  repeaters and, 158–59
  serendipity and, 162–65
  teach yourself, 157
  three-step error correction process, 159–61
Legal problems, 56–60
  forms needed, 59–60
  policies and procedure manual, 58–59
Loans. *See* Capital

M

Macroeconomics, 5, 81, 150, 200
Management failure, 86–106
  accounting problems and, 60–63
  bylaws and, 42–43
  expanding too quickly, 18
  financial problems and, 70–83
  highly detailed plans and, 20–21
  internal bickering and, 43
  lack of working capital and, 12
  legal problems and, 56–60
  nepotism and, 44
  organization and, 46–56
  partnerships and, 30–44
  plannning backward and, 21–22
  stock and, 38, 40–41, 43
  unrealistic plans and, 18

INDEX

Management functions, 86–103
  decision making and emotions, 95–97
  delegate responsibility, 90–92
  formalization of the business, 86, 87–90
  poor direction and control, 92–95
  reacting to events, 99–100
  self-discipline, 100, 179, 180–81
  what are they, 14, 86
Market survey, need for, 9–10
Merger(s), 122–38
  cash versus stock in, 131–32
  common mistakes the seller makes in a, 124
  employees and, 126, 128
  post-merger plans, 127, 128–30
  post-merger sales, 130–31
  professional negotiators for, 132–33
  reasons for, 123, 125–27, 136–37
  synergistic, 123
  time it takes for merger to occur, 134–35
  what happens to seller after, 124–25
  when should you sell, 135–36
  who are the buyers, 127–28, 133–34
  who sets price, 125
Mistakes:
  in business plans, 14–28
  financial, 70–83
  in going public, 141–53
  growth and, 106–19
  how to avoid making, iii
  learn from, 100–101, 156–66, 200–204
  management, 86–108
  in mergers, 122–38
  organization and, 46–56
  repeating, 101–2
  three-step error correction process, 159–61
"Mongolian horde," 114
Murphy's Law, 72

N

Napoleon, 6, 21
Negotiators, professional:
  used in mergers, 132–33
Nepotism, 44, 97–99

O

Operational mistakes. *See* Management functions
OPM (other people's money), 71
Orderly market, 152

Organization, 46–65
  mistakes in, 47
  no, 47–49
  organizing around special people, 52–54
  organizing in name only, 54–56
  rigid, 50–51
  too many changes in, 51–52
  too much, 49
Ownership problems, 40–41, 42–44

P

Paige, Satchel, 192
Partnerships, definition of, 30–31
Persistence:
  aggressiveness and, 178
  behavior at work versus behavior at home and, 177–78
  circumstances that affect, 174
  "comfort zone" and, 172
  discipline and, 179–83
  goals and, 177
  needed to start a business, 169–71
  poor judgment and, 168–69
  sales and, 175
  self-discipline and, 180–81
  supervising and, 175–76
Personnel, how to obtain, 35–36
  See also Employees
Planning. *See* Business plans
Policies and procedure manual, 58–59
Post-merger plans, 127, 128–30
Post-merger sales, 130–31
Pricing:
  going public and, 142–43
  raising prices, 110–11
  underpricing and effects on growth, 110
Profit:
  growth versus, 74–75, 112–13
  planning for, 18
  problems and, 68–83
Profit and Loss statement, keeping track of, 69–70
Progress reports:
  for employee evaluations, 94
  for feedback, 93
  how to create, 94
Proprietorship, definition of, 30
Prospectus, preparation of, 146–47
Prosperity:
  client relationships and your, 108–9
  growth and, 108–9
  how to obtain, 8

R

Record keeping, 69–70, 72–74
Rewards, risks versus, 8–10
Risks:
    rewards versus, 8–10
    serendipity and, 164

S

Sales and persistence, 175
SBA. *See* Small Business Administration
SEC (Securities and Exchange Commission):
    prospectuses and, 146
    trading on insider information and, 148
Securities and Exchange Commission. *See* SEC
Security, lack of job, 7–8
Seesaw management, 176
Selling of a company. *See* Merger(s)
Serendipity:
    being aware of, 163–64
    chance and preparation and, 164–65
    definition of, 162
    risk and, 164
Sexual harassment, 97
Shareholders:
    forming a coproration and, 33
    See also Going public
Shares:
    selling of shares to get start-up capital, 34
    See also Going public
Small business(es):
    economic factor of, 4
    number of, 4
    reasons for failure of, 12, 18, 20–21, 42–44, 47, 200
    risks versus rewards in a, 8–10
    time necessary to spend working for, 171–72
    types of, 30
Small business, qualities needed to start:
    aggressiveness, 178–79
    ambition, 172
    discipline, 179–80
    persistence and good judgment, 168–83

Small business, qualities needed to start (*cont.*)
    self-discipline, 180–81
    supervisory ability, 175–77
Small Business Administration (SBA):
    hotline to, 68
    purpose of, 6
Spending freely, 77–80
Statistics:
    economics and number of bankruptcies, 80
    failure rate of small businesses, 4, 5, 80
    number of bankruptcies, 5, 80
    number of new businesses started in 1981, 3
    number of small businesses, 4
Stock:
    buy/sell agreements and, 41–42
    cash versus stock in mergers, 131–32
    employees and, 36–38, 39
    ownership problems and, 40–41, 43
    types of, 36
    unregistered, 131
    See also Going public
Stock options, used to hire personnel, 35–36, 41
Straight line depreciation, 62
Success. *See* Prosperity
Supervising, importance of, 175–76
Synergistic merger, 123

T

Three-step error correction process, 159–61
Trading on insider information, 147–49

U

Undercapitalization, 70–72
Unemployment Compensation Insurance, 59
Unregistered stock, 131

W

Wall Street Journal, 3, 68, 129
Working capital. *See* capital